You make known to me the path of life; in Your presence there is fullness of joy; at Your right hand are pleasures forevermore.

Psalm 16:11 (ESV)

Renewed Joy

5 SIMPLE STEPS TO LASTING & POWERFUL JOY IN THE LORD

STEPHANIE PAGE

Contents

Introduction

I've Got The Joy!

"I've got the joy, joy, joy, joy down in my heart!!
Where?"

I remember singing that old Sunday School favorite as a young child while jumping around and clapping my hands in delight, eagerly anticipating the next opportunity to shout "WHERE?" at the top of my lungs.

Circumstances in life slowly robbed that joy from me. Once a carefree and easily delighted child, I woke up one day to find myself barely surviving. There was even a time when I did not want to live anymore.

Thank God that He rocked my world and awakened me to joy! I cannot wait to let you in on some incredible insights that God has taught me along the journey. *You do not have to live feeling discouraged.* You can have daily, powerful and lasting joy—guaranteed!

Happiness and joy have different definitions. Happiness is defined as: "feeling pleasure and enjoyment because of your life situation." Joy is defined as "a source or cause of great happiness: something or someone that gives joy to someone."[1] True joy is more than a feeling, more than just happiness. True joy comes from a source, one that remains constant, even when the feeling of happiness comes and goes. This book will examine the path that leads to the true source of joy!

True joy is both free and freeing. Keep reading.

Have you ever felt lonely, discouraged, or overwhelmed? Maybe all three simultaneously? Have you ever felt like you were going under, sinking, drowning in the deepest darkest part of a vast ocean? I have.

Friend, let me tell you this: If that is you, there is hope. I am throwing you a rope, a life-line of truth through this book. My life has been marked by many hard trials. I have weathered the storms of hurt, loss, disappointment, loneliness, change, financial difficulty, rejection, fear, infertility, miscarriage, chronic illness and more. In lonely, discouraging, and overwhelming times, I can testify of God's goodness and faithfulness through it all.

If you are looking for hope—for fresh joy—you are in the right place.

Join me as I introduce you to the 5 Steps to true, powerful and lasting Joy in the Lord. Together we will also discover Biblical tools to refresh our joy and live a life with direction, purpose and peace, even through life's daily challenges and storms. Many women have put these 5 Steps into practice and have experienced the resulting, ongoing joy in their lives. Please hear me when I tell you this: If you are struggling in any way and do not walk through these 5 Steps, your life will be full of uncertainty and empty of confident purpose.

Friend, many women walk through life claiming Christianity and a relationship with Jesus as their own, but they are living without joy. Broken, hungry, lonely women (in an ever-connected world) are aching for fulfillment in life—women who are panicked by the pace of this world, women obsessing over their bodies and carrying deep-rooted shame, women grieving broken marriages and prodigal children while wearily raising their grandchildren, women who have rejected faith in Jesus that they claimed as children or teens. I see women who are barely surviving, and yet if asked, "How are you?" they answer, "I'm fine," but their sad, tired eyes give away their secret pain.

Why?

What is happening to us as daughters of the King? I will tell you exactly what is happening. Satan is out to steal, kill and destroy our joy in the Lord. He wants to cripple our testimony and our impact for eternity. He wants to rip God's strength right out of our hands and he knows every distraction and diversion trick in the book.... But God!

One name for God in the Bible is Jehova-Jireh, The Lord Will Provide. The Great Provider sees every single moment of time and has every winning strategy for a joy-filled life in The Book, His Word! Women, I invite you right now to turn away from the lies of the world that call out, "We will make you happy!" Instead, turn toward your identity and calling in Christ Jesus because *we were made for more*. God has a plan for your life.

Can I get an AMEN?! Whew! Ladies, my hands are shaking as I furiously type these words. The almighty God has given us a perfect guide to joy in His Word, the Bible. I cannot wait to share God's goodness with you and what He has taught me in my life's journey through His Word. I desire that this book will help you, too, find your way to lasting and powerful joy. You can be set free from the chains of sin and live in the freedom, purpose and overwhelming hope of the Gospel—the hope of our salvation and eternity spent with Christ.

Dear woman, if you want to continue worshipping at the feet of idols—money, fame and attention, relationships, fashion, a fabulous home, the perfect figure (or the perfect Instagram feed for that matter), high achieving children or fabulous vacations—then you had better put this book down. But I will warn you—those idols will leave you empty, desperate and devastated because none of those things can *ultimately* satisfy you. *Guaranteed.*

You were made for more than feeling constantly overwhelmed in a fast-paced world. You were made for more than the feeling of persisting loneliness and discouragement.

Stick around! Read on!

> *"The joy of the Lord is your strength."*
> (Nehemiah 8:10)

My Gift To You

Before we dive into your first step toward joy, I have a special surprise for you. You did not know this was coming, but, friend, I want to overflow God's love into your life and give you more than you anticipated. Gifts are fun! Go right now to www.pageofjoy.com/bookgift and you can download a special gift. Trust me, you really do not want to miss this. People are loving it! In addition to your surprise, a free Renewed Joy study guide is available that will upgrade your journey through this book. It will also make referencing your notes and thoughts simple once you have finished reading, if you like to take notes.

Did you do it? I really want you to have this special, free gift while it is still available.

Yay! You have found your special gift and now we can move forward and discover joy together. Are you ready? I am. One, two, three... *GO*!

Redeemed

Once God saved by grace through faith, rejoice that your life is redeemed by the true and living God!

Chapter 1
Redeemed

The First Step to Joy: Salvation

"...That the payment for my sin was the precious
life He gave. But now He's alive and there's an
empty grave. And I know my Redeemer, He lives."

– Nicole C. Mullen[1]

A timid young woman, about thirteen years old, walked up in front of the crowd, trembling yet resolved, and declared her belief in Jesus and her desire to serve Him with her whole life. Her name was Stephanie Joy. That girl was me, of course.

I may not have known the entirety of the commitment I was making in that moment, but somehow I knew this: God is real, His Word is true and I wanted to follow Him wherever He would lead me. My heart, up until then, was brimming with fear, anxiety and longing. A painful and confusing childhood had left me in survival mode, treading the waters of school and life, anxiously desiring to *live with purpose* but not knowing where to find clear direction for life. Suddenly and yet gently, the beat of my heart and soul changed. I awakened to new life in Christ and breathed hope... purpose... peace...confidence... safety... joy! I have never been the same.

Do You Believe That God Is Real and His Word Is True?

Salvation is the first step toward lasting, eternal joy. Where are you on this journey, friend?

The Bible—God's very words—is compiled of 66 books written over about 1500 years by around 40 authors in three different languages and from three different continents, and it covers hundreds of topics. During this time in history, there were no light bulbs, much less the Internet and social media, yet every book aligns in complete harmony and no one was "tweeting" spoiler alerts to help keep each other's stories straight. Not only that, but the Bible predicted, or prophesied, many events that have actually been accurately fulfilled!

The Bible is stunningly cohesive and lacks contradiction because it was written by one flawless author—God. *"For no prophecy was ever produced by the will of man, but men spoke from God as they were carried along by the Holy Spirit"* (2 Peter 1:21). God breathed His words through men and gave us a true, living, powerful, inerrant, inspired and infallible gift. *That gift is the only perfect guide to life here on earth.* It was a perfect guide a hundred years ago and it will still be a perfect guide for hundreds of years to come, as Jesus said, *"Heaven and earth will pass away, but My words will not pass away"* (Luke 21:33).

Since the Bible Is True, What Does It Say About God?

The Bible begins by telling us that God is the Creator of the heavens and earth and all living things. As the only true God, He is fully good. God exists eternally in the form of Father, Son and Holy Spirit (often referred to as the Trinity). Sin—anything that we think, say or do that does not honor God—separates us from a holy God and demands justice.

for all have sinned and fall short of the glory of God, and are justified by His grace as a gift, through the redemption that is in Christ Jesus, whom God put forward as a propitiation by His blood, to be received by faith... (Romans 3:23-25)

People strive toward God or goodness through many forms of religion, but the one true God is unique because He mercifully reaches right down to save us. Jesus, God in the flesh, was born of the virgin Mary and lived a sinless life, though He faced temptation just like you and me. He took upon Himself the judgment that we deserve—death—because of our sin by dying on the cross in our place. After three days buried in a tomb, He rose from the dead, declaring victory over sin and death. This event actually happened!

The death and resurrection of Jesus Christ completely satisfies the death penalty that we deserve for our sins, *"for the wages of sin is death, but the free gift of God is eternal life in Christ Jesus our Lord"* (Romans 6:23). He freely offers us the gift of complete forgiveness and salvation so that we can spend eternity with Him in heaven. *"For God so loved the world, that He gave His only Son, that whoever believes in Him should not perish but have eternal life"* (John 3:16). What an amazing God, full of love and mercy! *"...But God shows His love for us in that while we were still sinners, Christ died for us"* (Romans 5:8). This is truly Good News!

Friend, God so loves you! As you take the step to believe in Him, tell God that you are sorry for the sins you have committed and repent of them, turning away from your sins. Tell Him you believe in what Jesus Christ did for your sins by His death, burial and resurrection. Accept the gift of salvation from the One who has the power to redeem your life.

Determine to follow Him with your life. In doing this, you are forgiven, redeemed by the power of His blood. You are then washed clean and restored to relationship with Him, assured of your home in heaven for eternity. Your life can now be filled with true purpose and hope.

God does not ultimately desire to punish you, but because He is perfect, and just, He cannot be in the presence of sin. When Jesus willingly offered Himself as a sacrifice, He broke that barrier between our sin and the presence of God. *The blood of Jesus His Son cleanses us from all sin"* (1 John 1:7). His death and resurrection made possible the relationship God truly desires to have with you—not to punish you but to draw near to you and wash you in His love.

Life is not just about being "good enough" to get to heaven. If we were able to be good enough, then why did God send Jesus to be born, live a sinless life and die in our place? Why did Jesus have to die? Remember Romans 3:23, *"For all have sinned and fall short of the glory of God."* We could never be good enough. To be good enough, we need to be perfect from birth to death. Thankfully, that is not God's plan for salvation!

Do you believe that God is real and His Word is true? Do you understand that He is pure and good and you cannot ever be good enough to reach His standard by your own merit? Do you see this incredible God who freely offers to restore you to relationship with Himself, forgiving all of your sins and creating an eternal home for you? If you have not asked Him to forgive you for your sins and to become Lord of your life, I urge you to do that now. You never know what tomorrow may bring.

Do not wait.

Plane Down in the Bering Sea

Following a week-long evangelistic and humanitarian aid trip to Lavrentiya, Russia, Dave and Barb Anderson, Cary Dietsche, Brian Brasher, Don Wharton and Pam Swedberg boarded an eight-seat Piper Navajo airplane that would take them back to the United States by flying over the Bering Sea. Dave Cochran, a missionary pilot with fifty years' experience, refueled the plane, packing the empty gas cans into its aisles. The plane took off on the long flight to Gambell, Alaska, where they would re-enter the United States.

From there the pilot would again take off and climb to 7,000 feet for the 45-minute flight to Nome. Some of the passengers began to doze off while reflecting on the amazing week of ministry that had occurred in this "end of the earth" region of Chukotka.

The story continues in Dave Anderson's words:

> My wife, Barb, sitting in the second row, couldn't take her eyes off the gas gauges. Uneasy, she prayed for God's protection. When the skies began to clear, Barb relaxed, but continued to watch the instrument panel silently.

> *Crash Landing*

> When the right engine sputtered, Barb jumped. The second sputter woke me up. Glancing out my window, I watched the propeller slow down, shake unsteadily, and stop. In the cockpit, Dave Cochran calmly switched on a pump to cross-feed fuel from the left engine to the right engine. Almost at the same instant, we all heard him radio to Nome, "Out of fuel on one tank...descending from seven thousand feet...seven souls on board."

> A few moments later, the left engine went dead. We were two miles from the nearest land—Sledge Island—and plummeting from 3,500 feet toward the frigid waters of the Bering Sea. Before we lost transmission with Nome, Dave was able to relay our position.

> We were all praying aloud now, especially for Dave. Even with 18,000 hours of airtime, nothing like this had ever happened to him. As long as our pilot didn't panic, we felt we had a chance.

> In seconds, Dave had made critical decisions: feathering the propellers to slow us down, concentrating on keeping the plane's nose up, not retracting the landing gear to minimize possible cart-wheeling. We watched out the windows as the plane began to skim and bounce off the four-foot waves.

The Piper Navajo's speed was 90 mph when we hit, sending a geyser of water heavenward. Amazingly, Dave kept the nose up as we careened another 300 feet through the water. Spinning 180 degrees, the crippled craft finally stopped, bobbing on the waves. Water immediately began pouring in.

Upon impact, Don Wharton hit the emergency window exit. Though his seat had been ripped from its frame as luggage catapulted against it, Cary Dietsche escaped through the rear door. There were no life jackets or rafts on board, but we were in luck. "Everyone grab a gas can," Dave yelled. In less than a minute, while we all clung to our five-gallon cans, the plane disappeared under the frigid water.

The youngest member of our group, Brian Brasher, began shouting, "God is our refuge and our strength; a very present help in trouble." We took turns reciting Scripture, calling out our locations every few seconds since the sea was carrying us away from the crash site. I tried to grab Barb, but she drifted out of reach.

Since we were in shock, at first the water seemed tolerable. We were all wearing light winter clothing. Thankfully, we were unaware of three things: the water temperature was 36 degrees, survival in that temperature is at best 15-20 minutes, and no one had ever survived a crash in the Bering Sea.

A Life-Saving Delay

An hour behind schedule, Bering Air pilot Terry Day was trying to make up time from St. Lawrence Island to Nome. Cruising at 2,000 feet above the open sea, he noticed something out of the corner of his eye. A white plume of water shooting up. In an instant, it was gone.

A whale spouting, Day thought. A few minutes later, his radio crackled. "Aircraft in difficulty...attempting a landing at Sledge Island...deviate [your course]...let me know if you spot the aircraft..."

The plume of water, Day remembered. Could it have been that plane hitting the water? Turning back and descending, he alerted his passengers of the detour.

In the water, we saw the plane approaching. Would he see us? Night was beginning to fall. The plane kept heading west, then disappeared. Miraculously, a few minutes later, the plane circled back. We waved and splashed, but couldn't keep it up long. We needed our energy to hold on to the gas cans.

A passenger looking out the window of the Bering Air taxi saw the commotion in the water and yelled at Day, "There's people down there!" Immediately, an Eskimo Christian on board began praying for our safety.

Day radioed Nome, "There are people in the water using some kind of flotation devices. But I don't have enough fuel to keep circling. I have to head back to Nome."

Just then, another voice broke into the transmission. Vic Olson, a pilot minutes away, volunteered to take over for Day. When he arrived, he dropped to 500 feet above us and circled.

In the water, we were beginning to feel the cold through our bones. Numb and shivering, we continued to encourage each other. "We're going to make it!" "They know we're here. Hold on!" Gripping the gas cans was becoming more difficult. We were all getting weaker. We knew we needed to be rescued soon.

Heroics In The Sky

At the Nome airport, the emergency call went out. Eric Penttila, a pilot for Evergreen Helicopters of Alaska, had originally planned to go salmon fishing that evening. But at the last minute, he changed his mind and was home when the phone call came. He contacted his friend and mechanic, Jerry Austin, and told him to meet him at the hangar where he kept his helicopter used for food and mail deliveries to isolated Alaskan villages. Just before takeoff, Randy Oles, a Nome firefighter and search-and-rescue veteran, also jumped on board. Twenty minutes later, they pinpointed Olson's circling Navajo. Scanning the water, they counted at least six people floating.

A geological survey helicopter piloted by Walter Greaves offered assistance. He and his passenger, Dave Miles, happened to be out testing a newly replaced altimeter. Penttila radioed his position and Greaves was on his way.

Seeing Penttila's helicopter, Barb cried out to the rest of us to hold on. Above us, the three men were shocked. "I can't believe they're actually alive," they admitted to each other. It was a race against the clock—and the cold—to keep us that way.

Barb noticed the helicopter had no pontoons; it would not be able to land on the water. Inside the chopper, the men were assessing what little rescue equipment they had. They would have to rely primarily on human strength.

Penttila's chopper slowly descended, hovering inches above Brian Brasher. Over the roar of the rotors, Brian directed them to Cary Dietsche. "Get him first." He was injured in the crash and said his legs were cramping.

Firefighter Randy Oles, balancing on one of the skids, watched Cary disappear under the water, forced down by the velocity of the helicopter's rotors. He leaned over and tapped him on the head. Cary was too weak to even raise his hand to help, but Oles grabbed his coat and pulled him to safety.

The Evergreen crew headed toward me. Oles again climbed onto the skid and grabbed my hand. Several times my fingers slipped. Between the sea's swells and the water spray kicked up by the helicopter's rotors, I felt like I was in a car wash. In a daring move, Penttila dipped the skid far enough into the water so I could get my leg on it. Grabbing my belt, Oles and Jerry Austin got me inside.

Not far off, Dave Cochran was in the late stages of hypothermia—drifting in and out of consciousness. Minutes earlier, he had let go of his gas can and was floating freely. His waterlogged coat began to drag him under. Oles and Austin, with a rope, both positioned themselves on the skid. Amazingly, after a few attempts, they were able to get the rope wrapped around Cochran. Pulling him up was another story; whenever they came close, a wave would hit Cochran and he'd disappear. Fortunately, the rope kept him connected.

Finally, the two rescuers resorted to another plan. Throwing the free end of the rope to Cary and me, they stayed outside the chopper, precariously holding on to Cochran and the skid.

Penttila lifted the helicopter and headed slowly for Sledge Island, two-and-a-half miles away. Cochran was half-dangling from the skid. Penttila gently put the chopper down on the island tundra, and Cary and I got out and wrapped the missionary pilot in a sleeping bag and stayed with him.

Walter Greaves and Dave Miles in the second helicopter were zeroing in on Barb. Miles sat on the skid and got his hands on her, but Barb's clothing made her a dead weight. No longer aided by a gas can, she would certainly drown.

After several attempts, Miles held on to a black strap anchored to the chopper, and edged his way to the end of the skid. When the strap began to give, Miles grabbed the helicopter's strut and Barb. Pulling her up, Miles locked Barb's head between his knees. With his back to the helicopter, he wrapped his legs tightly around her body, held Barb with one hand and the strut with the other. Barb's feet skimmed the water.

Reaching the island, Miles realized with horror that Barb was slipping. If she fell from this height on the rocks, she would certainly be killed. Signaling Greaves, they headed back to sea-fifty yards out. Barb wiggled loose because she was having difficulty breathing—Miles was holding her so tightly.

Hitting the water and sinking, Barb still managed to pray, "Oh, God, help me, my strength is gone." Struggling with her last bit of energy, she broke the surface, choking and gasping for air. When she tried to swim, there was nothing left. Her water-filled jacket became a lopsided flotation device, and Barb lay back, expecting to die.

A noise got her attention. Miles was swimming out to her. Clutching her coat once again, the two half-swam, half-stumbled to the rocky shore.

Meanwhile, Penttila's rescue team headed out for Pam Swedberg and Don Wharton. With effort, Swedberg got into the helicopter; Wharton dangled between Oles and Austin on the skid as they ascended 760 feet to the highest point on the island. There was no beach or shoreline to land on.

Greaves headed out to locate Brian Brasher.

The last survivor had drifted; after four passes over the area, Greaves spotted him. Hovering, Greaves waited for Penttila to return from Sledge Island. Brasher fought to keep his head above water as the lethargy of hypothermia set in. Fifteen minutes later, he was reunited with our group. He had been in the water sixty-five to seventy minutes. Ambulances were waiting for all of us at the Nome Airport for transport to the hospital. There, we were treated for hypothermia and released. Barb and Dave Cochran were kept another day.

In 1994, all of our rescuers were honored by the U.S. government. Eric Penttila, Walt Greaves, Terry Day, Vic Olson, Randy Olsen, and Jerry Austin each received the Distinguished Service Award from the Federal Aviation Administration. For his outstanding heroic efforts to save Barb, Dave Miles, a Canadian, was awarded the American Medal of Heroism. It was the first time a Canadian had ever received such an honor.

To this day, we can't get over the amazing series of small things that "happened" to fall in place on that day. Gas cans, late flights, available helicopters. Only God could have orchestrated such a miracle. His rescue from overwhelming circumstances is a constant reminder to us of his faithfulness.[2]

My dear mother-in-law, Kathy, was supposed to be on that plane. I believe God preserved her for many reasons, one being to love me and my family well and to influence our hearts for the glory of God. Pam Swedberg, one of the survivors of that plane crash, is a friend of ours. She makes the most delicious desserts, but that is not why God saved her (although it is a wonderful bonus). God has a specific purpose for her life and He spared her unto His glory.

God has a plan for your life too.

Don Wharton, one of the Bering Sea Plane Crash survivors reflects:

"Dealing with life's challenges is a matter of trusting God in all situations. Make no mistake about it, if we would have died in the crash, we would have still been rescued. Jesus Christ provided that rescue 2,000 years ago on Calvary. However, God didn't take us to heaven on August 13, 1993. He provided our rescue, perhaps so we could share the message that if God can rescue us, then He can rescue anyone. It won't be easy. You might not even be rescued in the way you want to be rescued or on your time schedule. But His Word is true when it says, *"Trust in the Lord with all your heart, and do not lean on your own understanding. In all your ways acknowledge Him, and He will make straight your paths."* (Proverbs 3:5-6).[3]

So, friend, have you been rescued? Have you believed in Jesus, the Son of God, repented of your sin and trusted in Him for salvation? Have you chosen to follow Him? (Learn more about following Jesus by reading the Gospel of John in the Bible.)

When those seven people were in the turbulent waters of the Bering Sea, they were desperately in need of a rescuer—they could not rescue themselves. Swimming to shore was not possible due to distance and the water's temperature. Each of us at one point or another lives in the turbulent waters of sin; we too need a Rescuer—we cannot get out of those waters and save ourselves. Do not put your confidence in any other way but Christ who is the Way. *"There is a way that seems right to a man, but its end is the way to death"* (Proverbs 14:12), but *"...if you confess with your mouth that Jesus is Lord and believe in your heart that God raised Him from the dead, you will be saved."* (Romans 10:9).

If you have already put your faith in Jesus but have somehow lost your joy in Him, and find yourself discouraged or broken, then I want you to think back to the first time you discovered His great love. Today, thank Him for all that He has done and for who He is and move forward. Take the time to delight yourself in the Lord and His gift of salvation—healing will come.

Whether you have been a believer for five minutes or five decades, the beautiful truth of our salvation through God's grace never grows old. *"For by grace you have been saved through faith. And this is not your own doing; it is the gift of God"* (Ephesians 2:8). Friend, once saved by grace through faith, rejoice that your life is redeemed by the true and living God!

> Amazing grace, how sweet the sound
> that saved a wretch like me!
> I once was lost but now I'm found
> was blind but now I see![4]

<u>The first step toward joy is to be redeemed by the grace of God!</u> Pray and thank God for saving you. Specifically thank Him for the changes that you have seen in your heart, and ask Him to help you to be faithful to Him and His Word as He continues to lead you through your life on earth for His glory.

Redeemed

Once saved by grace through faith, rejoice
that your life is redeemed by the true and living God!

Renewed

Upon salvation the Holy Spirit dwells inside of
you and produces the fruit of true joy in your heart and life!

Chapter 2
Renewed

The Second Step to Joy: Trust the Holy Spirit's Work in You

"The world is perishing for lack of the
knowledge of God and the Church is famishing
for want of His Presence."
– A.W. Tozer[1]

Once we trust God for salvation, the Holy Spirit comes to dwell inside of us. What an amazing truth! The Bible says that the Spirit of Him who raised Jesus from the dead lives inside of you and gives life to your body (Romans 8:11). We also read in Romans 8:1, *"There is therefore now no condemnation for those who are in Christ Jesus. For the law of the Spirit of life has set you free in Christ Jesus from the law of sin and death."*

So we now know that God's very Spirit lives in us upon our salvation, but does He have any other roles in our life? Absolutely. The Holy Spirit is fully God and is part of the Trinity (God the Father, God the Son and God the Holy Spirit). Genesis 1:2 tells us that the Spirit of God was present before creation. He helps us to understand the Gospel (1 Corinthians 2:12). He unifies the body of Christ (1 Corinthians 3:16, 12:12–13). The Bible also says that the Holy Spirit dwells in the children of God (Romans 8:14). He is powerful and has fellowship with us (2 Corinthians 13:14), and He strengthens your inner being with that power (Ephesians 3:16). He is our Helper and our Advocate (John 14:16, 26). He makes us holy, transforms us, and prompts us to worship (Galatians 4:6), and is our Teacher and Leader in following Christ (John 15:26, Galatians 5:16). God's Spirit in us produces fruit through our lives, including the fruit of joy!

Consider this definition of joy: "Joy is repeatedly shown to be the natural outcome of fellowship with God."[2] The Holy Spirit produces this incredible joy in us when our trust is rooted in God and His Word. Because our joy comes from Him, joy is not dependent on feelings or circumstances. This joy is confident, enduring, peaceful and filled with hope! *"In Thy presence is fullness of joy; in Thy right hand there are pleasures for evermore"* (Psalm 16:11, KJV). The Holy Spirit produces this incredible joy in us.

The Holy Spirit causes our joy-fruit to bloom. What fruit have you seen in your life as a result of the indwelling of the Holy Spirit? Patience? Self-control? Faithfulness? Joy? Gentleness? Love? Kindness? Peace? Goodness?

I recently repented when convicted of a lack of patience toward my children. The Holy Spirit showed me where I was trying to operate outside of His power, which was only causing frustration in our home. He helped me, and is still helping me, to learn gentleness and patience toward my children, even when they are knowingly naughty. My response was sin-driven instead of Spirit-driven. If you evaluate your heart and life and do not see the fruit of the Holy Spirit at work, I urge you to ask God to show you if sin is in your life. Release your white-knuckle grip on your favorite sins. Repent of your sin, be controlled by His Spirit and restored to joyful intimacy with God. Allow Him to produce the fruit of joy through your life as He has done in mine. *"But the fruit of the Spirit is love, joy, peace, patience, kindness, goodness, faithfulness, gentleness, self-control"* (Galatians 5:22-23a).

From the first day that I trusted Christ for salvation, the Holy Spirit began a new work within me. He protected me, guided me and comforted me. As God weaves the tapestry story of our lives, we will certainly all face hard trials, but if we have the joy of the Lord as our strength, we can still see fruits of the Spirit, even if we do not necessarily feel happy. The Holy Spirit has produced good fruit through my life even during hard times. He has the power to weave each "snag" along the way into a beautiful part of our story.

From the day that I repented and trusted Christ, fast forward twelve years to a clean and tidy living room where I sat, broken, on a sofa with my four-month-old baby asleep in his car seat and my loving husband at my side. A wise and Godly couple counseled me as I laboriously processed through piles and piles of confusion and pain in my heart that I had never before put into words. Something about having a child brings out the depths of childhood pains.

As a new mom, I began to see what God had intended for my life and what Satan had stolen. I grieved, immersed myself in the Word of God and processed as many memories as I could remember, though they were few. This dear couple helped me to understand some of the specific ways that God had designed me. As I learned God's truth about me, the Holy Spirit began to replace the shame and lies that I had been drowning under for so long. As I spoke aloud the heartbreaking circumstances that I had faced in life, those secret and confusing times suddenly lost the power of shame over me. God's Word, correctly applied and coupled with the power of the Spirit, flooded light and freedom into my soul. The girl who was sinking under heartache, sorrow, loss, shame and insecurity slowly began to rise above the waves, buoyed by grace, and my soul felt washed by God's glorious light of truth, freedom and love—true joy. The Holy Spirit began a healing work in me and I re-discovered the awesome ways of our one powerful God.

If you believe that every moment, every breath of your life, is powered by the Holy Spirit, even the overwhelming times of loneliness or discouragement, how does that change you going forward? Ephesians 3:20 tells us that God is able to do *immeasurably more than all we could ever ask or imagine, according to God's power that is at work within us.*

Despite joyful, Spirit-powered healing taking place in my life and the unfolding of deep and intimate times with Jesus, a miscarriage when my first child was about ten months old *threatened* to swallow me up with grief. I lay on my bathroom floor sobbing. Shaking, I wondered if my heart would ever beat right again. I ached and wailed for a time, and then the sobbing ebbed into a river of long, wet tears. My baby was dying inside of my body. Nothing has ever felt so sorrowful.

Maybe it was my smiley ten-month-old baby boy, a reflection of what was being lost, that amplified the pain. Sometimes knowing what you are losing makes it harder. Sometimes.

I have never, ever, longed for heaven the way I did after my baby went to live there. My heart ached and I wondered how... *how* could a good God use something so awful to bring glory to Himself? How many others have asked this question? Many. I still do not fully understand how, but He does bring glory to Himself through difficult circumstances, and it is pure and good that He does. I know unwaveringly that He is real and heaven is real and my baby is there now. And we can trust His plan.

God values my tears. *"You have taken account of my wanderings; Put my tears in Your bottle. Are they not in Your book?"* (Psalm 56:8, NASB). Another name for God found in the Bible is *El Roi*, Hebrew for "The God who sees you." He sees me and cares about my sorrow. His Spirit in me is my Comforter; His gentleness draws me into a peaceful trust of His ways, especially when I do not understand them. He sees you and values your tears, too.

The Holy Spirit within me was and is my Helper and Comforter. Despite the sorrow of loss, I know there is yet hope. I know that my baby's life mattered, even if it was barely a blip on our earthly calendar. When you do not understand God's ways, persevere and walk by faith, dependent on the strength of His Spirit in you. This is the joy of the Lord at work in you during difficult times.

In Genesis we see the story of Joseph, a man who walked by faith and persevered, even when he could not understand the overwhelming and painful circumstances in his life. Being sold into slavery by his brothers was obviously an evil act. However, we also see that this same horrible circumstance unfolded into providential provision and protection for *many* people. By being sold into slavery, Joseph eventually earned the position of an esteemed ruler with great power and influence.

> *When Joseph's brothers saw that their father was dead, they said, "What if Joseph carries a grudge against us and pays us back in full for all the wrong which we did to him?" So they sent word to Joseph, saying, "Your father commanded us before he died, saying, 'You are to say to Joseph, "I beg you, please forgive the transgression of your brothers and their sin, for they did you wrong."' Now, please forgive the transgression of the servants of the God of your father." And Joseph wept when they spoke to him. Then his brothers went and fell down before him [in confession]; then they said, "Behold, we are your servants (slaves)." But Joseph said to them, "Do not be afraid, for am I in the place of God? [Vengeance is His, not mine.]* **As for you, you meant evil against me, but God meant it for good in order to bring about this present outcome, that many people would be kept alive [as they are this day].** *So now, do not be afraid; I will provide for you and support you and your little ones."* **So he comforted them [giving them encouragement and hope] and spoke [with kindness] to their hearts.** (Genesis 50:15-21, AMP, bold emphasis mine.)

In Joseph's story, we clearly see God bring good out of evil. This life-saving truth kept me afloat: God, in His mercy and grace, has carried me through pain and sorrow before, so I can trust Him to do it again. He can produce good from my suffering by the power of the Holy Spirit at work in me.

Many theologians discuss "How can an ultimately good God allow evil in the world?" C.S. Lewis said:

> My argument against God was that the universe seemed so cruel and unjust. But how had I got the idea of just and unjust? A man does not call a line crooked unless he has

some idea of a straight line. What was I comparing this universe with when I called it unjust?[3]

While I may not argue the finer points of theology alongside great academic scholars, I do know one thing for certain: God values life! In His providence He allowed my baby's earthly life to end exactly when He intended, though sooner than I wanted. Yet I will trust Him and His timing.

> *For My thoughts are not your thoughts, neither are your ways My ways, declares the Lord. For as the heavens are higher than the earth, so are My ways higher than your ways and My thoughts than your thoughts.* (Isaiah 56:8-9)

Out of my sorrow has been born the Spirit's fruit of love as I have trusted God's ways, and because of it, I have been able to minister to others who are grieving a similar loss (or really, any loss).

May we respond to others with love by the strength of the Holy Spirit *despite our suffering* instead of responding from bitterness *because of our suffering*. May we have eyes to look to others' needs instead of focusing intently on our own trials. May we offer comfort to the wounded and grieving. May we offer encouragement and hope. May we offer kindness toward the hearts of others, ultimately for the glory of God. This blooming in our hearts that occurs from living by the Spirit produces the fruit of joyful love from our lives regardless of circumstances.

Friend, spend time in the Bible getting to know the Spirit who lives inside of you. Be encouraged, knowing that He who began a good work in you will complete it (Philippians 1:6). Pray and ask Him to teach you and to lead you through His Word. Thank God for the freedom and hope that comes with the gift of the Holy Spirit dwelling in us.

The joy that comes from living by the Spirit allows us to see beauty all around us—glittering sunlight glinting off morning dew, sparkling fresh-fallen snow, flowers softly bending, fluttering leaves in a soft breeze, and birds tweeting and twittering, flitting from branch to branch. There is joy to be had in every moment as we walk in peaceful trust of the Spirit at work within us, regardless of our circumstances.

The second step toward joy is crucial—allow the Holy Spirit to work through you. Pray and thank God for giving you the Holy Spirit. Praise Him for empowering you to love and do good works through Him. Thank God for leading you and for helping you to understand the Gospel by the Spirit.

Redeemed

Once saved by grace through faith, rejoice that your life is redeemed by the true and living God!

Renewed

Upon salvation the Holy Spirit dwells inside of you and produces the fruit of true joy in your heart and life!

Relationship

Abiding in the almighty God who will never leave you results in deeply satisfying joy!

Chapter 3
Relationship

The Third Step to Joy: Abide in the Word

"If you abide in Me, and My words abide in you, ask whatever you wish, and it will be done for you. By this my Father is glorified, that you bear much fruit and so prove to be My disciples. As the Father has loved Me, so have I loved you. Abide in my love. If you keep My commandments, you will abide in My love, just as I have kept my Father's commandments and abide in His love. These things I have spoken to you, that My joy may be in you, and that your joy may be full."
(John 15:7-11)

I slid down the bumpy textured wall and landed on the cold tiled floor where I sat and sobbed for at least an hour (Dramatic much?). "They're moving? I'll never find another friend like her again." Amidst hiccups and sobs, I grieved the loss of a dear friend. She was not the first or the last. Over the course of two years, I lost eight close friends. They all moved far away.

Each time I poured myself out to build a new relationship, soon the phone would ring or a text would beep in: "I'm moving away." I began to joke that if anyone disliked living in Alaska they should befriend me and they would quickly find themselves a one-way ticket to anywhere else! But underneath the jokes, loneliness ached.

My heart longed for a forever friend who would not reject me or leave me behind. Though I knew that each friend moved away for good reasons, somehow I felt the sting of rejection each time. It ripped the scab off of old childhood wounds, and the pain ran deep. Little did I know that God would use those feelings of loss and loneliness to lead me toward unexpected joy. That almost seems impossible until you read more about what I discovered along the way...

Our Greatest Relationship

I am a Christian, the Holy Spirit lives in me, so what now? Have you ever felt that way? You are not alone. In the midst of busy lives and unexpected trials, we can easily choose to set aside the relationship with God that we once cherished. However, let me urge you, friend, do not forsake spending time with Christ, growing in Him and living by His power as He calls you to live. You only have one life to live.

> Give me Father, a purpose deep,
> In joy or sorrow Thy word to keep;
> Faithful and true what e'er the strife,
> Pleasing Thee in my daily life;
> Only one life, 'twill soon be past,
> Only what's done for Christ will last.[1]

What does that relationship with God look like practically in day-to-day life? Why do I want a close relationship with God? *"So Jesus said to the Jews who had believed Him, 'If you abide in My Word, you are truly My disciples, and you will know the truth, and the truth will set you free'"* (John 8:31-32). To be a disciple, Jesus instructs us to abide in His word. Strong's Concordance describes the word "abide" in this way:

> ménō, men'-o; a primary verb; to stay (in a given place, state, relation or expectancy): — abide, continue, dwell, endure, be present, remain, stand, tarry.[2]

We grow in our Christian faith, discover what God wants us to do and get to know our loving God by spending time with Him in His Word and in prayer. Time! The Word of God is a true and living book that will change your life. Read it, memorize key passages, meditate on what you have read and memorized.

Write down special verses and place them around your home or workplace to help you remember God's Word throughout the day. (If you have not already, go to www.pageofjoy.com/bookgift to download the free set of watercolor Bible verse cards that I have made for you.) As I began placing verses next to my bed, on my refrigerator and inside cupboard doors, my relationship with God was strengthened and my loneliness lessened. I discovered a new level of God's love for me. I began to see that I had a forever friend all along—Jesus (John 15:14-15). I continue to keep Bible verses throughout my home today.

God's Word never becomes old or irrelevant. It is the Bread of Life that nourishes your soul. Nourishes! I need that.

> Nourish: to provide (someone or something) with food and other things that are needed to live, be healthy, etc. To cause (something) to develop or grow stronger.[3]

As we come to know God more through His Word, we are nourished and made healthy and strong. Joy!

Psalm 19 tells us that God's Word revives your soul. It builds wisdom, keeps you from sin, helps you discern, comforts you in affliction and so much more. Read Psalm 119 to see the benefits of living by God's Word.

Let's dive into the Bible, friend! Savor its truth. Ask the Holy Spirit who dwells in you to teach you God's precepts for life and give you the strength to obey them. Jesus said in John 15:14, *"You are My friends if you do what I command you."* Obeying God's Word is what draws us into deeper relationship with Him, taking away our loneliness and replacing it with joy.

When you are making a decision, go to the Word of God. When you are faced with a controversial cultural trend, go to the Word of God. When you are uncertain, go to the Word of God. When you are lonely, go to the Word of God. When you are broken, go to the Word of God. If you are lost, go to the Word of God.

In Psalm 119:111, David says, *"Your testimonies are my heritage forever, for they are the joy of my heart."* God calls David "a man after My heart" in Acts 13:22. He was acquainted with both sin and pain, and yet he sings of his joy in the Lord. When we treasure God's Word, listen to His voice and follow it, we find great joy!

In the midst of grieving the loss of special friendships, I discovered that God alone could fully satisfy my desires for relationship. Through reading His Word, I began to know Him more and trust His character. When we read verses like *"He heals the brokenhearted and binds up their wounds"* (Psalm 147:3), or *"He determines the number of the stars; He gives to all of them their names. Great is our Lord, and abundant in power; His understanding is beyond measure"* (Psalm 147:4-5), we are filled with peaceful trust and moved to express joyful gratitude to the God who will never leave us nor forsake us (Hebrews 13:5).

So, friend, join me as we seek to be fully satisfied in knowing the almighty God! As we do what God instructs us to do in the Bible, He will produce fruit through our lives.

> *I am the vine; you are the branches. Whoever abides in Me and I in him, he it is that bears much fruit, for apart from Me you can do nothing. ...By this my Father is glorified, that you bear much fruit and so prove to be My disciples."*
> (John 15:5-8)

Do you see that? Abiding in Jesus (the Word) brings forth fruit and joy in your life, and is a mark of a true disciple of Christ.

Evidence or fruit of the Spirit at work in your life is called holiness. *"But as He who called you is holy, you also be holy in all your conduct..."* (1 Peter 1:15). That which is holy is sacred, consecrated to God.[4] Holiness is the conduct befitting those who are separated from sin and set apart to God. *"Strive for peace with everyone, and for the holiness without which no one will see the Lord"* (Hebrews 12:14). Living a holy life pleases the Lord. So, persevere! The process of being made holy is called *sanctification*. Sanctification does not happen overnight, but rather takes time and dedication. Carve out time in your day to be with Him.

In addition to satisfying joy, another fruit of abiding in Him is a growing love for other people, even those hard-to-love people. John 15:12 tells us *"This is My commandment, that you love one another as I have loved you."* How did Jesus love us? He died for us while we were still sinners. Verses thirteen to fourteen go on to say, *"Greater love has no one than this, that someone lay down his life for his friends. You are My friends if you do what I command you."* Our close friendship with Jesus involves obedience to His commands, including his command to love others as He has loved us.

What does it look like to love others as He has loved us? Start looking around and ask God to show you someone who is needy. It may not show in their outward appearance. Who needs to be generously blessed, served, heard or prayed for? When you open your eyes to the needs around you, the opportunities to serve can wash over you like an overwhelming flood. Go to the Lord in prayer and ask Him what *He* wants you to do. Start by helping just one person as God brings her to mind. We have the opportunity to love people around us by the power and strength of God. Whoa, that is radical! I'll say that again: *We have the opportunity to love people around us by the power and strength of God*... even if those people hurt us... even if they might leave us... even if they are radically different from us.

> *For you were called to freedom, brothers. Only do not use your freedom as an opportunity for the flesh, but through love serve one another. For the whole law is fulfilled in one word: "You shall love your neighbor as yourself."* (Galatians 5:13-14)

What would your life look like if you loved each person you came into contact with by the power of God? Begin to pray for those people now. You may be surprised to see how God moves not only in that person's life, but also in your own heart posture toward them.

As the fruit of the Spirit blossoms in your life, you will find it impossible to hide the beautiful transformative power at work in you. The natural next step is to tell everyone what God has done in you. *"But you will receive power when the Holy Spirit has come upon you, and you will be My witnesses..."* (Acts 1:8). In fact, as believers in Jesus Christ, we have a very specific job to do. Jesus spoke the Great Commission to eleven of His disciples:

> *All authority in heaven and on earth has been given to Me. Go therefore and make disciples of all nations, baptizing them in the name of the Father and of the Son and of the Holy Spirit, teaching them to observe all that I have commanded you. And behold, I am with you always, to the end of the age.* (Matthew 28:18-20)

Our natural response to God's transformative work should be telling others about Jesus.

Did you catch the last part of the verse above? Jesus does not just send you out to get to work. No, friend, He never leaves you. He is with you always. Not only that, but that hole in your heart that longs for relationship was carved out by God and is satisfied in relationship with Him. He lovingly built relationship with other people into our commissioning. Go and tell the Good News and make disciples!

Our lives have purpose—to glorify God! Joy comes as you spend time diligently seeking to know Him. Joy comes as you abide in Him and His Word. Joy comes when you obey Him, bringing glory to His name as you walk in holiness and love those around you with His powerful love.

Yes, I still miss my dear friends who have moved away, but instead of wallowing in the depths of loneliness, I am allowing my heart to be filled and satisfied by the God who never leaves me or forsakes me. I am filled with joy in ongoing, abiding, relationship with God.

<u>Abiding in relationship with God through prayer and knowing His Word is the third step toward joy!</u> Pray and ask God to fill you with a desire for intimacy with Him, that you will develop a deep hunger for His Word. Ask Him to help you to be holy. Thank Him for always being with you. Ask Him to show you how to love those around you with His love. Ask Him to help you to identify areas where you are enabling sin, idolizing others or being unloving. Thank Him for giving you the Perfect Example of love and for empowering you to love well.

Redeemed

Once saved by grace through faith, rejoice that your life is redeemed by the true and living God!

Renewed

Upon salvation the Holy Spirit dwells inside of you and produces the fruit of true joy in your heart and life!

Relationship

Abiding in the almighty God who will never leave you results in deeply satisfying joy!

AND

Re-purposed

Instead of living for ourselves, we now joyfully reach out for the sake of evangelism and discipleship!

Chapter 4

Repurposed

The Fourth Step to Joy: Reach out for the Sake of Evangelism and Discipleship

After being saved by grace and seeking Godly discipleship in our walks with Christ, we will naturally see the need to then share the work God has done in us with those who have not heard the Good News. Sharing the Good News, though, does not always come naturally. We must diligently equip ourselves, powered by the Holy Spirit, to share that Good News with those who have not heard. *"One generation shall commend Your works to another, and shall declare Your mighty acts"* (Psalm 145:4). We must ask the Spirit to ready our hearts and minds to teach new believers and those younger in the faith.

This learning and then teaching cycle is a clear directive to believers throughout the Bible (see more in Titus 2). For example, in the first four books of the New Testament (Matthew, Mark, Luke and John), we see a clear example of the first disciples learning from Jesus and then going out to spread the Good News to the world. The disciples followed Him and learned from Him, all the way up to the day He was crucified. When Jesus reappeared to the disciples after His resurrection, He instructed them to *"Go therefore and make disciples of all nations..."* (Matthew 28:19). Those instructions are for us too.

One summer I had the opportunity to join some dear women at a beautiful cabin in a remote Alaskan village. We prayed, worshipped God, ate delicious food, talked and joyfully laughed. A few days into the retreat, my grief over years of infertility spilled out and, through tears—possibly through hiccups—I asked them to pray for me. This group of women flocked around me with hands on my shoulders and tears in their eyes, kneeling on the hardwood floor as they bathed me in prayer. That moment was holy and precious. God did not answer my pleading for another baby in that instant, but He moved in my heart and showed me the power of a loving community and the joyous gift that we, as women especially, can have with one another. Our joy does not hinge on other people, but our joy can certainly be enhanced by them. Those women followed Jesus' command to make disciples by embracing me in love and prayer, walking with me in my struggles and helping point my eyes back to Him.

Experiencing the love and kindness of Godly women has taught me the importance of community firsthand. These relationships have taught me to be more gracious, patient, understanding, thoughtful, respectful, diligent, creative and brave. Engaging with other women in my community has shown me the value in reaching out to others instead of waiting for someone to reach out to me. I have pondered that sometimes what seems like a small gift offered by a friend is, in reality, a huge sacrifice of love from their place in life. Everyone needs help, and none of us knows everything. Even the glossy women who appear to "have it all together" have pain and questions and fear. Outside of Jesus, there is no quick fix to any issue or relationship. When in community, we can find wisdom in the white-haired women of the Word (Titus 2:3-5). However, nothing satisfies our longings except for God Himself. It is good to treasure friendships in their seasons but not hold a white-knuckle grip of expectation on them. When we enjoy the gift of friendship from God with thankfulness, it brings great joy. When we look to other people to fulfill our needs and desires, their friendship becomes a joy-diminishing idol. God-honoring community draws people in and points them to the Lord, the author of our joy.

I am so grateful for the different friends and mentors that have walked with me and poured love into me as I have grappled with trials in life. God has provided wise and kind women to speak into my life, and He is showing me through them how to reach out and share His love with others. The same can be true for you as well. It is such a joy to share His goodness with other people through evangelism as well as Bible study, discipleship and corporate worship.

> *And let us consider how to stir up one another to love and good works, not neglecting to meet together, as is the habit of some, but encouraging one another, and all the more as you see the Day drawing near."* (Hebrews 10:24-25)

The Church

God designed His church, the body of Christ, to operate in unity. You can see this playing out across the globe. Local churches are gathering together to learn about God, to worship Him and to mobilize service and outreach for the glory of God.

However, the enemy of God (Satan) wants to destroy the church and every good intention God has for it. Sadly, we have seen, again and again, people leveraging the church for personal gain; leaders who fall into moral corruption; abuse and neglect of the needy and hurting; and a lack of authentic worship and service powered by the Holy Spirit. May we never forget that the local church is made up of sinners, like you and me, who are saved but not perfect. But God! He accomplishes His purpose through the *true* church again and again as He wills. As The Jesus Storybook Bible said it, "This is God's battle and God always wins His battles!"[1]

Friend, if you have been wounded somehow regarding Christian fellowship and community, I am so sad for your pain and I want to offer this encouragement: God cares about you! He cares about the church as a whole and He designed for us to gather in community for good reasons. You may need to work through specific healing regarding the wounds in your heart by seeking Godly counsel—a hard but important step, especially if you have encountered trust issues with spiritual leadership. Trust God's Word when He says not to neglect the community of His church.

You can find pastors and Godly leaders who take very seriously the job that God has given them, and who resemble this verse: *"Remember your leaders, those who spoke to you the Word of God. Consider the outcome of their way of life, and imitate their faith"* (Hebrews 13:7). I have had the privilege of growing up in a church with a wonderful pastor, watching not only his life but the lives of his wife and children as well. Their family has been a light of God's love and faithfulness to me through the years. Their long-term commitment to our church has been especially comforting as I have grappled personally with authoritative trust issues. Good church leaders are out there. If you are not already part of a church body led by solid Biblically-minded leaders, I encourage you to find one.

The church exists to serve God; the church does not exist to serve us. We must lay aside our own sinful desire for the church merely to serve us. If the worship does not fit your style, or the women's ministry is not reaching your deep emotional "needs," or the mission committee chose to serve a different organization than the one that you passionately recommended supporting, consider this verse: *"And they devoted themselves to the apostles' teaching and the fellowship, to the breaking of bread and the prayers"* (Acts 2:42). Can the same be said of you? Are you devoted to the teaching and fellowship of a local church? Love, diligence and faithfulness are much more important than getting your own way. Let's be Spirit-fueled, Scripture-directed, Christ-focused and other-oriented in our times together.

Christ has adopted us as His children into the family of God, each with gifts to serve His people and the world (Romans 12:3-8). Remember—what He calls you to, He equips you for. So be joyfully bold and courageous! Pray and ask God what it looks like to be a part of your local church body. *"Until I come, devote yourself to the public reading of Scripture, to exhortation, to teaching"* (1 Timothy 4:13). Find a church community that reveres the Word of God and teaches what is *true* versus teaching what is merely entertaining. *"For the time is coming when people will not endure sound teaching, but having itching ears they will accumulate for themselves teachers to suit their own passions..." (2 Timothy 4:3).* It is much easier to find an entertaining but theologically shallow church these days than to find one that reveres the Word of God as inerrant, relevant and true. Do not settle for a church that provides mere entertainment, void of sound teaching, instruction, and exhortation.

Learn what the Bible says about unity among believers and God's heart for us to serve the orphans and the widows, to reach the hopeless and the lost, to feed and clothe the poor and the needy (Romans 12), and then, empowered and led by the Spirit, go and serve. Give generously as the Spirit leads and genuinely commit to prayer. The saying is true—"The ones who serve are blessed more than those they serve." *"Religion that is pure and undefiled before God, the Father, is this: to visit orphans and widows in their affliction, and to keep oneself unstained from the world"* (James 1:27). Look at each moment throughout your day, each encounter with another person, as an opportunity to show the love of God. Spread His joy!

As you mature in the Word, become part of a community of believers and receive discipleship from Godly mentors, you will begin to see that God also designed you to disciple others. When Jesus first sent His disciples out to make disciples, *"...He showed them His hands and side. The disciples were overjoyed when they saw the Lord. Again Jesus said, 'Peace be with you! As the Father has sent me, I am sending you'"* (John 20:20–22). Jesus showed His disciples the transformation that took place in Him, and it brought the disciples joy and peace. His disciples then went and shared about Jesus and the transformation that took place in their own lives, again bringing joy and peace to others.

Go preach the Gospel to people who do not yet have the freedom and salvation that Christ offers. Tell them what He has done in you. Build kind and loving friendships with people, and let God's light shine through you as you joyfully proclaim the miraculous work He is doing in you. The thought of doing this may make your knees knock and hands tremble, but offer that discomfort to God as an act of worship and ask Him to strengthen you to do what is right and say what is true in His eyes.

We are rescued and then we are repurposed into "rescuers," ones who bring the message of the ultimate Rescuer and show people the only way out of their sin and its ultimate consequence (see the directive in Matthew 28:18-20). What if the helicopter pilots and passengers had chosen not to risk their lives in order to rescue the drowning people bobbing in and out of the crashing waves that day in the frigid Bering Sea? Imagine going home after deciding not to try and reach down to save them. Imagine seeing the tears on the cheeks of the families who just lost their loved ones—drowned at sea. You are surrounded by others who are at risk of drowning. Thankfully, the pilots and passengers chose to reach out and help. Will you?

We can offer the Life-Saver to those who will perish without Him. Friend, if we have this joyful news that has changed our lives, how can we not throw it out to everyone? How can we not try to give every single person the Life-Saver that is the Gospel of Jesus Christ when we know it is the only way to be saved?

> A rescuer is afraid—but he doesn't let his fear decide what he does. A spiritual rescuer disregards his fear to give someone he knows a chance to live forever instead of die forever. Your prayer to God to open your mouth is essentially a prayer for spiritual courage—the kind that doesn't let fear decide what you do and believes that God is going to give you everything you need in the process.[2]

Pray for spiritual courage and watch as God answers by using you to encourage and draw others to Himself.

I recently attended a baby shower. The room was packed with smiling women all joyfully delighting in blessing this brand new mother. I had the opportunity to speak with a few women about Jesus and what He is doing in my heart and life, which was exhilarating, but it made my heart thump and my legs tremble with nervousness. Though sometimes we are afraid of offending someone or creating awkwardness, press on by the power of the Spirit!

The Holy Spirit led me as I spoke with one woman who continually resorted to "I'm fine," but eventually opened up a little more and even had tears rolling down her cheeks. She shared some of the deep pain she has endured, confessing that she knew about God in her head but needed healing in her heart. Her words reminded me of a convicting phrase that my pastor likes to bring up now and then: "Many people miss heaven by eighteen inches. They know God in their *head* but never let Him change their *hearts*." I shared with her that God is gracious and merciful, willing to forgive her of her sins and heal her deepest pain, and that God could bring about great joy in her heart and life no matter what trials she has endured, just as He has done for me. I threw her the Lifeline; I directed her to the Rescuer.

I do not know what God has done or will do in her heart since our talk, but I do know that without the enabling of the Holy Spirit, I would have fumbled that conversation. Thankfully, God is ever faithful, *because of His love for that woman*, and He helped me speak encouraging truth to her heart. I have her name written down and plan to continue praying for her.

> *According to the grace of God given to me, like a skilled master builder I laid a foundation, and someone else is building upon it. Let each one take care how he builds upon it. For no one can lay a foundation other than that which is laid, which is Jesus Christ.* (1 Corinthians 3:10)

You may not always be able to know if the person committed her life to Jesus Christ or reached true healing or victory over a struggle, trial or sin, but that does not mean that your words and actions in her life were not impactful. God often uses a team of people to bring a person to Him. Sometimes you may lay the foundation; sometimes you may build upon it.

Wherever you go, keep your eyes open for people in need of encouragement. There is no shortage of pain and sorrow in this world. The plane crash victims struggling against impending hypothermia and crashing waves in the icy Bering Sea knew they needed rescuing. When you look around at the people in your life, do you assume that because someone does not display an obvious awareness of her need for soul-rescue that she is too hardened of heart or unreachable? Are you only willing to share the Gospel comfortably and eagerly when someone asks you to? You must set aside your own hesitations in order to offer the Good News of Jesus Christ to everyone—even those who do not yet know they need rescuing.

In addition to telling people the Gospel, reach out to the ones who are young in their faith and encourage them on this journey. Bearing witness and testifying to the work that God is doing in and around you is a powerful way to point peoples' eyes to Jesus. *"In the same way, let your light shine before others, so that they may see your good works and give glory to your Father who is in heaven"* (Matthew 5:16). Let's flood this dark world with God-powered light!

Friend, obedience to God in the areas of mentorship and evangelism allows much fruit to be produced through our lives. Discover the incredible joy that results from choosing to obey faithfully and courageously. Once you recognize that you are loved beyond understanding by the God who hung the stars, how can you not be joyously filled to overflowing with the desire to tell people about Him?

<u>Reaching out with the goal of loving encouragement, evangelism and discipleship is the vital fourth step toward joy!</u> Praise God for offering you the free gift of eternal life and the opportunity to spread His message to others. Pray and ask God to give you eternal eyes—eyes that see each person as a soul in need of salvation. Ask for courage to speak according to God's will. Pray for those who seem unreachable. Thank God for empowering you to spread the Gospel joyfully.

Redeemed

Once saved by grace through faith, rejoice
that your life is redeemed by the true and living God!

Renewed

Upon salvation the Holy Spirit dwells inside of
you and produces the fruit of true joy in your heart and life!

Relationship

Abiding in the almighty God who will
never leave you results in deeply satisfying joy!

Re-purposed

Instead of living for ourselves, we now joyfully
reach out for the sake of evangelism and discipleship!

Re-focus

Giving thanks to God in all things
is the path to lasting joy.

Chapter 5
Re-Focus

The Fifth Step to Joy: Give Thanks in All Things

"Being joyful isn't what makes you grateful.
Being grateful is what makes you joyful."
– Ann Voskamp[1]

In the last four chapters, we have examined practices that nurture joy. But, how is it possible to have joy when a crisis arises?

As you journey through life, you will face hard times. Now, please do not put this book down! I promise there is hope. The Bible says that we will face trials of many kinds. In fact, Scripture goes so far as to say: *"Count it all joy, my brothers, when you meet trials of various kinds...."* (James 1:2). It is possible to have joy through the trials.

The Bible gives us the remedy for despair when we face trials. *"Give thanks in all circumstances; for this is the will of God in Christ Jesus for you"* (1 Thessalonians 5:18). We can choose to be thankful, even in the midst of hardship. When you choose gratitude, your focus shifts from your circumstances to your God, on Whom you can depend. Joy results as you walk in gratitude by faith in the One who is trustworthy.

Though it seems contrary to our natural response in the midst of hardship, giving thanks is a path to restored joy. This response has proven to be true for me. Through various trials, God taught me that He is trustworthy and faithful. He has given me a powerful tool that enables joy, even in the midst of difficulty—gratitude.

The Lord is My Shepherd, I Shall Not Want

Standing nervously beside my teacher's desk in a dimly lit classroom, I quoted the passage. I can still hear my small, first grade voice timidly finding its way through each verse.

The 23rd Psalm has been a meaningful reminder of the Good Shepherd throughout my life, especially in recent years. At just twenty-eight years old, after five years of working closely with my doctor, my body shut down, which forced me to face my symptoms and articulate them in a clearer way. At her recommendation, I diligently followed a treatment regimen for thyroid and vitamin deficiencies, allergies and hormones, and weight loss, and participated in a restricted diet, IV therapies, and more. Finally, she handed me this list of symptoms:

> Extreme fatigue and weakness
> Muscle and joint aches and pains
> Chronic headaches
> Sore throat, swollen glands, and periodic fevers and chills
> Numbness and tingling of the extremities
> Cognitive dysfunction (brain fog)
> Insomnia

Tears began to roll down my cheeks. I reminded myself, *"He makes me lie down in green pastures. He leads me beside still waters. He restores my soul. He leads me in paths of righteousness for His name's sake"* (Psalm 23:2-3). My doctor speculates that, along with other contributing factors, essential hormones developed incorrectly during my childhood due to overwhelming amounts of adrenaline. As a result, my body is not functioning on "all cylinders."

Facing the "why" of our suffering can tempt us to turn to bitterness and despair, but as believers in Jesus Christ, we have the opportunity to instead focus on the "Who."

> *Rejoice in the Lord always; again I will say, rejoice. Let your reasonableness be known to everyone. The Lord is at hand; do not be anxious about anything, but in everything*

by prayer and supplication with thanksgiving let your requests be made known to God. And the peace of God, which surpasses all understanding, will guard your hearts and your minds in Christ Jesus. (Philippians 4:4-7)

The peace of God, which He freely gives if we only ask, is so much better than knowing the "why" for our suffering. The Lord is at hand!

When we focus on the "Who" of our suffering, we will be able to give thanks. Jehovah-Raah is yet another name for God found in the Bible, and it means "the Lord my Shepherd." *"I am the Good Shepherd. I know My own and My own know Me, just as the Father knows Me and I know the Father; and I lay down My life for the sheep"* (John 10:14-15). We can always trust Jehovah-Raah to guide and protect us in His sovereignty, regardless of our circumstances. Because He is trustworthy and faithful to us, we always have an opportunity to give thanks. *There is always, always something to be grateful for.*

Reflecting on my life, I am grateful for God's hand of protection and His mercy. Though I was once a timid and broken little girl, I discovered true joy on the day I received salvation that remains unshaken, regardless of the earthly pain encountered thereafter. He grounded my faith and trust in Himself alone. I see the way He put a song in my heart and filled me with joy. I see His faithful shepherding throughout each choice, each circumstance. For example, God led me to my husband, who is a kind and gentle man of faith. I rejoice in my suffering because God has been trustworthy and faithful regardless of my circumstances.

In His mercy, God has allowed suffering in my life so that I might be refined by my circumstances and also encourage others who are facing trials, *for His name's sake.* I choose to focus on the One who leads me. I am thankful for the One who is always with me, the One who restores my soul. Taking my focus off of difficulties and placing it on Him inspires gratitude and great joy to spring forth from my heart. Friend, I encourage you to re-focus your heart and mind too!

"Even though I walk through the valley of the shadow of death, I will fear no evil, for You are with me; Your rod and Your staff, they comfort me" (Psalm 23:4). Through the valley of the shadow of death...words that were once just rhythmic syllables during a first grade classroom recitation became reality.

Many times, I have had to drag myself up the stairs, pulling on the railing as it creaked in complaint, because each step sent sharp pain throughout my whole body. I would forget important things. My husband would often speak to me, and then I would suddenly snap out of a thick brain fog and realize I had not heard a word he said...and he knew it. I sometimes could not pick up my own babies, and I had three children under the age of five. I could not push a vacuum, lift a full trash bag or stand to load the dishwasher. Like an elderly woman, I would slowly roll out of bed in the morning and walk, arched in pain, waiting for my stiff and aching body to warm up enough to straighten upright. If I tried to push through the tiredness and pain, I would collapse into tears and be rendered useless for long periods of time. I was exhausted *all...the...time*. And yet, many nights I could not sleep. At times, the screaming pain felt unbearable.

I have been ill for most of my life. Because that level of continual, physical pain was all I had known, I thought that was just how life was. Honestly, before we identified my illness, I assumed that everyone else fought similar physical battles and that I was just failing to overcome them with a smile. The words "Be strong!" "Push through!" and mostly, "You're such a failure!" were tracks playing on repeat in my mind. I felt hopeless. I needed to re-focus my mind and create a new track to play on repeat—one that was uplifting instead of defeating.

In the midst of the most difficult struggles, sometimes our biggest obstacle to joy is our own thoughts. When your mind is a swirling battlefield, here are some practical tools you can use to get your thoughts under control and move forward on your path to joy:

1. Say "NO" or "STOP" out loud. Recognize the negative thoughts that are simmering in your mind and *"take every thought captive to obey Christ"* (2 Corinthians 10:5b). Speaking out loud is a powerful way to help you overcome this mental battle.

2. Begin to read Scripture aloud or quote verses from memory. Psalm 103 is a wonderful place to start. However, consider the struggle you are engaged in and find specific Scriptures to help you. Are you facing a problem with another person or are you struggling against old temptations? Begin reading aloud in Colossians 3:1-17. God's Word is alive and powerful. Committing His Word to memory will encourage your heart and strengthen your faith. *"The sword of the Spirit, which is the Word of God"* (Ephesians 6:17b) is a powerful weapon.

3. Sing praises to God. A dear, gray-haired woman of the Word likes to say, "Praise makes Satan flee!" Praise God for who He is and what He has done in your life. Express gratitude to the Lord for the ways you have seen Him carrying you through the struggle.

Any time circumstances, feelings, or discouraging thoughts threaten to knock you off course, return to these practical tools. Though I battled discouragement, weakness and pain, God was with me and He gave me wisdom *in the midst of my suffering.* In my situation, rather than beating myself up for failing, gratitude was the answer. Sure, I could not always serve my loved ones the way that I wanted to, but I had the opportunity to practice resting in and obeying God's will. After all, He was allowing my illness, so I knew I could trust Him to show me *His* way to serve my family. Great joy comes in knowing that He is gentle and faithful and you can trust Him, even when—especially when—life does not look the way you hoped it would.

There were days when I lost hope, but He was still with me. His Word was a comfort to me. In a moment of desperation, I felt God's prompting to go back to my doctor yet again (a three-hour drive!). Nervously sitting beside the desk in my doctor's office, I read through the list of symptoms and it left me breathless. My doctor had a diagnosis: Chronic Fatigue and Fibromyalgia. *This is me*, I thought. Relief and hope surged through me. Something is so freeing about finally being able to name the "enemy." Once you know what you are battling against, you can apply the right strategy.

The enemy, whatever yours may be, does not separate us from God. He never changes and never leaves us.

> *You prepare a table before me in the presence of my enemies; You anoint my head with oil; my cup overflows. Surely goodness and mercy shall follow me all the days of my life...* (Psalm 23:5-6)

God is present with us every day, not just on our good days. Sharing from this portion in Psalm 23, Jonathan Parnell says,

> Yes, even through the affliction. Even through the valley. Even through the grave. God's goodness and steadfast love—God's unswerving faithfulness—will pursue me to the uttermost.[2]

We do not have to wait for the hardship to be over to experience the love of God. He meets us in the midst of our trials and fills us with joy.

So, how can we honestly count difficulties as joy? Here is where you find the joy:

> *Count it all joy, my brothers, when you meet trials of various kinds, for you know that the testing of your faith produces steadfastness. And let steadfastness have its full effect, that you may be perfect and complete, lacking in nothing.* (James 1:2-4)

The word *steadfastness* is translated from the Greek word *hypomonē*, meaning, "patience, enduring, steadfast waiting and perseverance."[3] In enduring trials for a righteous cause, Christ helps us to become more like Himself. I can count it all joy that in every moment, I am able to give thanks to God, who can bring good out of every circumstance.

In a Psalm about the steadfast love of the Lord for us, His people, we are called to *"Enter His gates with thanksgiving, and His courts with praise! Give thanks to Him; bless His name"* (Psalm 100:4). Did you see that? Read that verse again. We enter into His presence through gates of thanksgiving! Fullness of joy is found in His presence. So let's walk through those gates with thanksgiving and find full joy.

For me, in the midst of chronic illness, counting difficulties as joy sounds like this:

> Thank You God, for giving me *wisdom* to love, nurture and serve my family. Thank You for *strengthening* me to delete the pride in my heart and reach out for help. Thank You for *leading* me to find the help that I needed in order to heal and be strengthened physically. Thank You for *allowing* me to see improvements in my health recently. Thank you for who You are and for being with me every step of the way.

Practicing daily gratitude, writing down what I am grateful for one by one, reinforces the joy of God's provision and presence today. Remembering what He has done strengthens my trust in Him and fills my heart with joy.

However, friends, I will tell you that He does not always resolve our suffering this side of eternity. But you know what? He offers something better. *"I will never leave you or forsake you"* (Hebrews 13:5). As a young and vulnerable child, God was with me. Even at my darkest hour, God was with me. He is with me now and I can trust Him. Believers, when you face trials of any kind, even if you do not find freedom from your suffering, He is with you. I can tell you that no matter what season of life you are facing, He will keep His promise to be with you always. I am grateful to God for that! Are you?

"...And I shall dwell in the house of the Lord forever" (Psalm 23:6). Living in heaven with our Savior for eternity is our true hope. I can hardly wait. Until then, the King—my Father, Comforter, Healer, Master, Friend and Shepherd—is with me here, even in my suffering. Our focus during times of trial is Christ and spending eternity with God. Be encouraged.

> *So we do not lose heart. Though our outer self is wasting away, our inner self is being renewed day by day. For this light momentary affliction is preparing for us an eternal weight of glory beyond all comparison, as we look not to the things that are seen but to the things that are unseen. For the things that are seen are transient, but the things that are unseen are eternal.* (2 Corinthians 4:16-18)

When Paul wrote these verses, he was in the midst of incredibly difficult persecution. Paul was able to see the bigger picture, that in light of eternity, our hardships on this earth are "light and momentary."

No matter what you are facing, God remains the same. He is faithful, unchanging and good. He is with you and you can trust your Good Shepherd—Jehovah-Raah. Because you can trust Him, you have the opportunity to practice gratitude in every moment. Gratitude turns your eyes toward the Giver of every good thing and helps you realize that every single day is a gift. Joy springs forth in our lives as we continue to put gratitude into practice.

<u>Giving thanks in all things is the fifth essential step to live out lasting joy!</u> Pray and thank God for all He has provided for you. Praise Him for being the Creator of every good thing and for bringing good even out of pain and suffering. Ask Him to open your eyes to the gifts He has given you each and every day. Thank the One who has given you each day as a gift.

Chapter 6
Endurance

Run with Endurance for the Joy Set Before Us!

*Therefore, since we are surrounded by so great a
cloud of witnesses, let us also lay aside every weight,
and sin which clings so closely, and let us run with
endurance the race that is set before us, looking to
Jesus, the Founder and Perfecter of our faith, who for
the joy that was set before Him endured the cross,
despising the shame, and is seated at the right hand
of the throne of God. (Hebrews 12:1-2)*

I was recently sitting with my toes buried in soft, warm, green grass near my six-month-old twin babies, watching my four-year-old jump happily on a big trampoline. My husband walked up after returning from a day of work. You know that moment when suddenly your stomach drops shortly before bad news arrives? Somehow the feeling gets there before the actual announcement? Oh yeah. That happened. He had a smile on his face—he always does—but somehow the tightness around the corners of his mouth must have given it away. "Job lay-offs..."

The intense reality of caring for twin babies, my newly diagnosed and expensive chronic illness, our son's fifth birthday approaching, holidays looming ahead and the impending arrival of Alaskan winter (along with increased utility bills) all started to swirl in my head. What would we do? The progress in healing I had made, the hope I had for "smooth sailing" for a while after so many trials...all that vanished with those two words: "laid off."

You know what? The 5 Steps to Joy described in this book are exactly what I used to delete the enemy's opportunity to wiggle into my heart and fill it with fear and doubt. These steps work! Remembering that I am redeemed, empowered by the Holy Spirit, guided by the ever-true Word of God, and surrounded by Godly mentors and friends, I moved forward knowing that I could give thanks in the midst of all things. I held onto confident joy! Jesus said, *"I have said these things to you, that in Me you may have peace. In the world you will have tribulation. But take heart; I have overcome the world"* (John 16:33). He remains my source of joy no matter what life brings. Jesus is my joy.

God's purpose for our lives will unfold through good times and bad. He uses the painful trials to refine us and purify us—to make us more like Him. (What an honor He bestows upon us!) Friend, one of the most powerful lessons I have learned in my trials of life is that trying to escape hardship is futile. However, it is extremely valuable to endure under righteous suffering (suffering that is to the glory of God and not a consequence of personal sin) and allow God to bring His good out of it. He is doing His work daily, right inside my heart, in the midst of hard things. Oh yes, I definitely still want to jump ship sometimes when friction begins, but the more I know Him (the more He reveals Himself to me through His Word and prayer), the more easily I can rest in His goodness regardless of my circumstances. I can rest content in His plan for my life, and the result is enduring joy.

Cultural and technological distractions can entangle us just like trials in life, like losing a job. We must commit to managing our time so that we can keep an intimate relationship with God and not give away our joy to sin. Living here on earth has nothing to do with buying all of the things we desire and being constantly comfortable and entertained. Do you believe that? Sometimes I slip back into believing that satisfaction will come from those things...a cute new outfit, an entertaining show, a cleaner and larger home, or impressive job titles and glossy vacations. Lies. Remember, none of those things bring lasting and powerful joy. Those lies that so easily distract us must be exposed.

How about you? Is there an area of your life that is being *merely entertained* by the world around you instead of being *fully satisfied* by the joy of knowing God more? Pray and ask God to show you. When I prayed through this area of my life, I was convicted of spending too much time watching certain TV shows. Though at first it was hard to let go, I found great joy in spending more time with Him once I chose to obey.

Daily disciplines help us to run the race with endurance as we continue on our faith journey. None of these works qualify you for salvation, but salvation comes by grace through faith in God alone. Remembering that each person is different, let's explore some areas of self-discipline that can help fertilize the soil of spiritual growth.

Before I became a mother, I thought words like "free spirit," "independent" and "spontaneous" were the ideal characteristics of any person. When my first child was born, I discovered the amazing, beautiful and joyfully *freeing* power of routine, consistency and discipline. In fact, ask a wildly successful businessperson, and he will likely affirm this truth: self-discipline leads to more abundant success in business and in life.

Consider this verse.

> *Have nothing to do with irreverent, silly myths. Rather train yourself for Godliness; for while bodily training is of some value, Godliness is of value in every way, as it holds promise for the present life and also for the life to come.* (1 Timothy 4:7-8)

When an athlete is training to compete, she cannot eat junk food and sit on the couch all day, every day, and still expect to show up to the race and beat the best competitors in the world. No way! Each habit and choice in training leads to the ability to be a strong competitor and even win the race. How much sleep a person gets, when she exercises, how she trains and every bite she eats adds up to success.

Training is a lifestyle. Spiritual growth should not be compartmentalized to Sunday morning church alone, but instead should be integrated into every moment of your life. 2 Peter 1:5-11 emphasizes this truth and shows us that diligence strengthens endurance.

> *For this very reason, make every effort to supplement your faith with virtue, and virtue with knowledge, and knowledge with self-control, and self-control with steadfastness, and steadfastness with Godliness, and Godliness with brotherly affection, and brotherly affection with love. For if these qualities are yours and are increasing, they keep you from being ineffective or unfruitful in the knowledge of our Lord Jesus Christ. For whoever lacks these qualities is so nearsighted that he is blind, having forgotten that he was cleansed from his former sins. Therefore, brothers, be all the more diligent to confirm your calling and election, for if you practice these qualities you will never fall. For in this way there will be richly provided for you an entrance into the eternal kingdom of our Lord and Savior Jesus Christ.*
> (2 Peter 1:3-11)

A.W. Tozer wrote, "Complacency is a deadly foe of all spiritual growth."[1] Diligently seek the Lord and you will experience true and lasting joy, even in the face of trials and distractions.

In an effort to guard against distractions that cripple us on our path to joy, we need to implement tactics to strengthen the areas in which we want to be successful. When I asked older and wiser women of faith to share their daily spiritual habits and disciplines, they offered inspiring thoughts. I encourage you to prayerfully consider implementing some of their ideas into your daily life. I will share some with you:

Kathy shares:

Because I can so easily fall back on worldly wisdom—I begin each day by reading one chapter in Proverbs, seeking to build God's wisdom into my heart. In the summer I change it up and read through the Psalms a couple of times. It's always fresh and new!!

Because I get anxious and somewhat overwhelmed at times, I've just started a new habit of beginning my day *"casting all of my cares upon Him for He cares for you"* (I Peter 5:7). I then tell Him I will live today depending on Him, His strength and leading and not my own. I ask Him to guide my priorities. If I remember, I also like to do this at night before going to sleep.

Because I so easily forget—because I sin, am prone to wander, so desperately need God, want to know Him and become like Christ as a Christ follower—I absolutely LOVE to dig into His Word daily—read it, study it, look up word meanings, memorize it and meditate on it. I begin this time asking the Holy Spirit to be my Teacher and Guide and to open my eyes to see what He wants me to learn and apply. I do not want to just read it, but have ears to hear what He is saying to me, then to listen to His voice and obey it. This renews my mind in His truth, nourishes and restores my soul, rejoices and gives hope to my heart, and is a light to my path. It is indeed more valuable than gold and sweeter than honey!!! It is never old, boring or dull to me!

Because of my task-oriented brain and the busyness of our culture/lives, I have begun to set aside Sunday as a day of rest ("The Rest of God" is the book that helped me with this). This is not a legalistic, self-righteous thing, but a gift from God to take a break from the woulda-shoulda-couldas, the taskmasters in my brain. It's a time of rest for my mind, body, heart and soul. If it works out, after church I like to nap, memorize some verses, do a Bible study, take a walk, and read in a Christian book.

MarJean shares:

Over the last eight years or so, before I get out of bed, every single morning, and sometimes while I'm still awakening, I fervently pray the words of this hymn by Edwin Hatch (1835-1889):

Breathe on me breath of God, fill me with life anew, that I may love what Thou dost love and do what Thou wouldst do.

Breathe on me breath of God, until my heart is pure, until with Thee I will one will to do and to endure.

Breathe on me breath of God till I am wholly Thine, till all this earthly part of me, glows with Thy fire divine.

I pray this hymn to remember I can do nothing without Him (Jn. 15:5), but I can do all things through Christ who strengthens me (Phil. 4:13). After Jesus' resurrection he said, "'As the Father has sent me, even, so send I you.' And when he had said this, he breathed on them, and said to them, 'Receive the Holy Spirit'" (Jn. 20:21-22). I pray this hymn because I want to invoke the Holy Spirit to come into my life and transform it. All I am and all I have comes through His life within me, His "breath" fills and moves me through all circumstances.

"Breathe" written by Marie Barnett in 2003 so describes my own heart's desire, "This is the air I breathe. . . Your holy presence Living in me. . . And I, I'm desperate for You. And I, I'm lost without You. . . You are my daily bread. This is my daily bread. . . Your very Word Spoken to me." Therefore, my spiritual disciplines consist of praying hymns, communing with the Lord through His Word, and prayer journaling.

Renee shares:

I find that I grow the most when I am involved in a Bible study and/or systematic Bible reading (Dr. Horner's program, the One Year Bible, etc.). I also need quiet personal time for focused prayer. Praying aloud helps keep my mind from wandering. Memorizing Scripture passages is also important in occupying my mind with truth. Sometimes I like to sit at the piano and play and sing praises to God. I really enjoy being alone with God, and I remember the struggle as a young mother of finding time in my day for even a quick devotional. When you are blessed with a husband who recognizes that desire and makes sure you have that private time with God, you are very thankful for him!

Rhee shares:

1. A few friends and I meet every other Monday morning to pray together. We also text each other during the week if we have a prayer or praise to share.

2. I try to pray continually throughout the day as the Lord brings people or situations to my mind.

3. I haven't done this for a while, but need to get back in the habit: taking a walk and praying out loud. I feel so close to the Lord when I do that.

4. Listen to Scripture or sermons throughout the day at home or while I'm driving.

5. Read a book that teaches about spiritual things to my husband in the evening.

Terry shares:

I read the Word each morning before doing anything else, pray regularly (including often in the night and early morning while still in bed), attend church regularly to participate in corporate worship and hearing the Word taught, and talk with my husband about any questions I have about Scripture. Memorizing Scripture is really important, but I have not done well with this for a while. I plan to begin again soon.

I really enjoyed the humble yet inspiring answers these real women shared with me. While I only gave you a sampling of their answers, you likely found an idea or two to try out in your own daily walk with Christ.

Now friend, I feel it is important to remind you that there is no magic formula for growing in and living for Christ. I admit to you that I struggled for years with not meeting my own self-created expectation of the "perfectly disciplined Christian." In these years of raising small children, I rarely wake early and sit with my Bible while having intimate time with Jesus. As the seasons in my life have changed, I have discovered that there is not only one specific routine that we must follow to abide in Christ. I am inspired to look continually for more creative ways to spend quality time with God. He gives me wisdom and peace as I seek to abide continually in Him throughout my day.

Whatever disciplines you adopt in order to pursue a deeper relationship with the Lord, be sure that you are spending time in His Word daily. Sometimes I sit for an hour and read during my kids' naptime, hungrily devouring God's Word for spiritual nourishment, and some days I read a verse or two and think on it throughout the day. Keeping Scripture cards around my home inspires me to think on God's Word often. (I have made a free set of Bible verse cards for you. If you have not already, go to www. pageofjoy.com/ bookgift to claim yours.) I often glean Biblical encouragement from Bible teachers and speakers online (such as Ann Voskamp, Lysa TerKeurst, Jennifer Rothschild, Joni Eareckson Tada, Kay Arthur, Jennie Allen and more). These are just a few ideas of ways to be in the Word daily.

In addition to being in the Word, I enjoy listening to and singing worship songs. Quality worship music with God-honoring lyrics inspires me to stop in the midst of cooking dinner and with hands raised and eyes closed, I sing praise to my heavenly Father. This precious time of worship is an overflow of God's renewed joy in me. I recently opened my eyes after an impromptu worship session and caught a glimpse of my five-year-old son with hands raised and eyes closed singing along. Talk about worship! I thought my heart would burst with joy.

Spend time thinking about God and praising Him for who He is. Walking outdoors and seeing God's creation always helps to center my heart on God's omnipresence, omnipotence and omniscience. Tiny wildflowers, beautiful trees, clouds gliding overhead, water lapping on the shore...ahhhhh! Heavenly! Feeling small in this great big world is humbling, but also brings great peace when you trust the One who orchestrates all of the waves crashing, wind blowing, butterflies flitting, birds soaring, and streams gurgling.

Get involved in a Christian community. Listening to sermons from my local pastor and joining in or leading small group Bible studies is a powerful area for growth in my life. Being a part of community the way God instructs us to is not always easy and is often imperfect, but it is oh-so valuable.

Interacting with other believers and hearing from them how God is at work in their lives is a great way to help you draw closer to God. Learning from other Christian women has become a great source of joy in my life. Ask Godly women you know to share some of their favorite spiritual practices with you. Pray and ask God for wisdom, perhaps as A.W. Tozer prayed:

> O God, I have tasted Thy goodness, and it has both satisfied me and made me thirsty for more. I am painfully conscious of my need of further grace. I am ashamed of my lack of desire. O God, the Triune God, I want to want Thee; I long to be filled with longing; I thirst to be made more thirsty still. Show me Thy glory, I pray Thee, so that I may know Thee indeed. Begin in mercy a new work of love within me. Say to my soul, "Rise up, my love, my fair one, and come away." Then give me grace to rise and follow Thee up from this.[2]

So friend, as you run this race called life, throw aside the weight of distraction and implement daily disciplines to strengthen and nurture your spiritual growth. Run with steadfast and persevering endurance, looking to Jesus for the joy set before you, like the apostle Paul, who said, "*I press on toward the goal for the prize of the upward call of God in Christ Jesus*" (Philippians 3:14).

Redeemed

Once saved by grace through faith, rejoice
that your life is redeemed by the true and living God!

Renewed

Upon salvation the Holy Spirit dwells inside of
you and produces the fruit of true joy in your heart and life!

Relationship

Abiding in the almighty God who will
never leave you results in deeply satisfying joy!

Re-purposed

Instead of living for ourselves, we now joyfully
reach out for the sake of evangelism and discipleship!

Re-focus

Giving thanks to God in all things
is the path to lasting joy.

Chapter 7
Pulling It All Together

Throughout this book we discovered the 5 Steps to Joy, five Biblical truths that lead us out of discouragement, distraction and depression to full joy in the Lord. Let's take a brief look at them once again and pull these 5 Steps to Joy together in our minds.

1. Recognize the joy of being Redeemed!

Once saved by grace through faith, rejoice that your life is redeemed by the true and living God.

By faith, you can receive the free gift of salvation through Jesus Christ and be forgiven of your sins, redeemed by the power of His blood shed for you. Tell God that you are sorry for the sins you have committed, repent, believe in His death and resurrection and accept the gift of salvation from the One who has the power to redeem your life. You can be washed clean and restored to relationship with Him, assured of your home in heaven for eternity. Your life can be filled with true purpose and hope. Friend, do not close this book without putting your trust in God alone.

> *For by grace you have been saved through faith.*
> *And this is not your own doing; it is the gift of God.*
> (Ephesians 2:8)

2. You are being Renewed by the power of the Holy Spirit!

Upon salvation, the Holy Spirit dwells inside of you and produces the fruit of true joy in your heart and life.

The Holy Spirit plays a vital role in our daily joy. He convicts us of sin as we journey through life. As we confess our sins to God, He faithfully forgives (1 John 1:9). Joy results as we are forgiven! As we then yield to the Spirit's control and live under His constant guidance and influence, He produces His fruit of joy in and through our lives. As we allow the Spirit to work in and through us, He strengthens us with power in the inner man (Ephesians 3:16). This Spirit-led daily walk is essential for lasting joy.

> *Now to Him who is able to do far more abundantly than all that we ask or think, according to the power at work within us, to Him be glory in the church and in Christ Jesus throughout all generations, forever and ever. Amen.*
> *(Ephesians 3:20-21)*

3. Our greatest *Relationship*!

Abiding relationship with the Almighty God who will never leave you results in deeply satisfying joy.

No relationship on earth can fill the hole designed to be filled by the Great God of the universe. He alone can satisfy your desires for intimate relationship. Knowing that He made you, loves you and desires relationship with you brings satisfying joy. When you abide in Him and seek to know Him more through the Bible, His perfect love joyously overflows into all of your other relationships.

> *I am the vine; you are the branches. Whoever abides in Me and I in him, he it is that bears much fruit, for apart from Me you can do nothing.*
> *(John 15:5)*

4. The joy of a life that is *Repurposed* from self-focused to selfless.

Instead of living for ourselves, we now joyfully reach out to serve those around us for the sake of evangelism and discipleship.

Our lives can be compared to *Fixer-Upper*, the fabulous HGTV show that features Christian couple Chip and Joanna Gaines as they "take the worst house in the neighborhood" and turn it into a dreamy gathering place. Our old lives were a mess without Christ, but now, by the power of the Holy Spirit, we welcome people into our lives just like a warm and welcoming Joanna Gaines design.

It would be a shame if Joanna decorated a stunning home and then the new owners locked the doors and no one stepped foot inside it ever again for fear of dirtying its pristine condition. A home is a place made for gathering, loving and living. Similarly, our lives are created for relationship (with God and people); for opportunity to testify to one another of God's works; to encourage one another by using our gifts; for discipleship, accountability and mentoring; and for meeting one another's needs to the glory of God. We can be an army of God's light to this dark world if we lay aside our selfish desires and reach out with His love. Entering into community creates opportunity for encouragement, evangelism and discipleship.

> *And they devoted themselves to the apostles' teaching and*
> *the fellowship, to the breaking of bread and the prayers.*
> *(Acts 2:42)*

5. **Re-Focus** your heart and find joy in any circumstance.

Giving thanks to God in all things is the path to continual and lasting joy.

The Bible shows us the path to joy on happy days and on hard days: *"give thanks in all circumstances; for this is the will of God in Christ Jesus for you"* (1 Thessalonians 5:18). As you choose gratitude, your focus shifts from circumstances to the God on whom you can depend. Joy results as you walk in gratitude by faith in the One who is trustworthy.

> *Count it all joy, my brothers, when you meet trials of various*
> *kinds, for you know that the testing of your faith produces*

steadfastness. And let steadfastness have its full effect, that you may be perfect and complete, lacking in nothing.
(James 1:2-4)

John 15:7-11 pulls together the 5 Steps to Joy beautifully:

If you abide in Me, and My words abide in you, ask whatever you wish, and it will be done for you. By this My Father is glorified, that you bear much fruit and so prove to be My disciples. As the Father has loved Me, so have I loved you. Abide in My love. If you keep My commandments, you will abide in My love, just as I have kept my Father's commandments and abide in His love. These things I have spoken to you, that My joy may be in you, and that your joy may be full. (John 15:7-11)

When we abide in Jesus and walk by the Spirit, we will bear much fruit, prove to be disciples of Jesus and glorify God. We abide in His love by keeping His commandments. He spoke those words to us in the Bible *"that My joy may be in you, and that your joy may be full."*

A.W. Tozer said,

If we cooperate with Him in loving obedience, God will manifest Himself to us, and that manifestation will be the difference between a nominal Christian life and a life radiant with the light of His face.[1]

This, my friend, is the result of true joy—living life with the radiant light of the Lord.

Chapter 8
How to Lose Your Joy

"Restlessness and impatience change nothing except our peace and joy. Peace does not dwell in outward things, but in the heart prepared to wait trustfully and quietly on Him who has all things safely in His hands."
– Elisabeth Elliot[1]

Maybe it was stolen or maybe you threw it away. Did you wake up one morning and wonder where your joy went? Was it a shocking phone call? Was it a slow goodbye? Yeah. I have been there too.

Discontentment

As I walked down a beautiful dirt road lined with evergreen and Aspen trees, I was impressed with the thought that all of the trees, flowers and grasses grow upwards... ^^^^^^^^^^^^^^^^^^^^^^^^^^^^ They are like arrows pointing straight to heaven. I could not shake the imagery all day long. Everywhere I went, I was reminded that life holds more than just the here and now, and even the trees seem to know it.

Funny how I have walked that same dirt road while twisting over in my heart how I wished it were a different road, a prettier road, a road with better weather. Yep, there is my sin of discontentment laid right out on the page for you to see.

It is much easier for me to think about how lovely it would be to live in Hawaii than it is for me to exercise thankfulness for the gifts that I have here in Alaska. This is especially true for me when I cannot even simply step outside because of the sheer ice that waits just beyond my doorstep. When my kids are stir-crazy with cabin fever in the dark of winter, and we have run out of creative ideas to make the most of those long and dark eight months, I can so easily slip into daydream mode.

Thoughts begin to take root in my mind, like, "Think of your happy place." That phrase is a "cute" technique we enjoy employing in our culture, but a deceptive one, because suddenly my sunny daydream makes the gray winter seem even darker and my discontentment grows larger.

Listen up: take action and stop the lust for "different" dead in its tracks for the sake of joy!

> *...for I have learned in whatever situation I am to be content. I know how to be brought low, and I know how to abound. In any and every circumstance, I have learned the secret of facing plenty and hunger, abundance and need. I can do all things through Him who strengthens me."* (Philippians 4:11b-13)

Sin and joy cannot co-exist in your heart. The sin of discontentment extinguishes joy faster than a deluge of rain snuffs out a campfire and soaks your freshly made s'mores. It is said that "Comparison is the thief of joy,"[2] but I would add that discontentment, lust, and even complacency are also thieves of joy.

All of these things—comparison, discontentment, lust, complacency, and more—are signals that sin is taking root in your heart. In one of the most spiritually impactful books that I have read, "Idol Lies," author Dee Brestin illustrates how to identify idolatry in your heart using a conversation she exchanged with her friend, Leslie.

Dee: I asked Leslie to give an everyday example from her life.

Leslie: I'm in line at the store, in a hurry, and the clerk is slow. I feel myself getting angry, irritated. That's the signal from my body that my idol is operating, that I am worshipping something besides God, that I am exchanging the truth of God for a lie.

Dee: So what do you do?

Leslie: I ask myself what the idol is. In this case it is myself, my agenda, my schedule.

Dee: Then what?

Leslie: First, confess. I am not more important than this clerk. I am not loving her as God does. Then I must repent, asking Him to help me turn and love this clerk. I want to worship the Creator instead of the idol of myself and my own agenda.

Dee: Leslie's illustration shows how change must embrace both parts of the Gospel: repentance and faith. She had to see her sin and repent but then also move toward the clerk in love, if only in her thought life.[3]

This example that Dee shared has impacted me greatly. Friend, when you sense the signals of sin taking root in your heart, do not delay! Repent and respond in love for the sake of your joy in the Lord and for the sake of His ultimate glory through your life. Allowing your heart to nurture sin and build up idols will make you weak. Your light will dim, your love will become selfish, your testimony will be muddied. In my case, the sin of discontentment crippled my attitude of gratitude and was a dark cloud over our entire household.

> Joy isn't a function of what happens.
> Joy is a function of what I think.
> Joy is a function of how I thank.
> – Ann Voskamp[4]

Complacency

Another familiar foe is a really sneaky enemy. In fact, she can become your best friend without you even recognizing her presence—complacency.

Life is busy. This world is unbelievably full—more so than ever! Family life, ministry life, school, constant Internet access, entertainment choices, traveling... So much accessibility has created a high demand for performance. We feel the pressure to do it all, and do it all with Pinterest perfection. After all, if you can then you should, right? *As we become overwhelmed with the demands of day-to-day life, we begin to set aside the intimacy with Jesus that once filled us with such great joy.* Ann Voskamp states it well: "Busy is a choice. Stress is a choice. Joy is a choice. Choose well."[5]

There are two types of "overwhelmed." The first is an unfortunate and familiar experience for many women today. This type buries us under fear, guilt, expectations, temptation and distraction. When we become complacent in our journey with Christ, this type of overwhelmed can quickly smother our intentionality as we seek to know God more and abide in Him.

The second type of overwhelmed is God's kind that makes you fly! God's mercy *overwhelms*, swelling around you, lifting you into the air to soar on wings like eagles, to walk and not grow weary, to run and not grow faint. His grace *overwhelms* and strengthens you to joyfully soar (from Isaiah 40:28-31). Do not allow complacency and distraction to lure you away from the true source of joy. Do not allow intimacy with God and time in His Word to slip away.

When Shock Knocks

When the shock of grief and loss hits like a tidal wave, there is no shame in a lack of bubbly happy feelings. Do not confuse feelings with joy. Remember the difference between happiness and joy from the introduction? Merriam Webster's dictionary defines happiness as: "*feeling* pleasure and enjoyment because of your life, situation." In comparison, joy is described as: "a *source* or cause of great happiness; something or *someone that gives joy* to someone."[6] As we trust God and believe the truth of His Word, that confident, enduring, peaceful, hopeful joy results in spite of our circumstances.

In addition, God brings good from every situation unto His glory. Elisabeth Elliot said,

> I am not a theologian or a scholar, but I am very aware of the fact that pain is necessary to all of us. In my own life, I think I can honestly say that out of the deepest pain has come the strongest conviction of the presence of God and the love of God.[7]

Grief is a journey. Grieving can make you feel like joy has been stolen, but there is always joy in knowing that the faithful and unchanging God will walk with you all the way through your pain.

As you journey through times of sadness, continue to press into the Lord, regardless of how you are feeling. This may look different as you pass through different stages of grief, from simply surviving all the way to establishing a "new normal." Remember, He is faithful and keeps His promises.

When grief and fear threaten to rob your joy, remember these wise words from Elisabeth Elliot:

> Where does your security lie? Is God your refuge, your hiding place, your stronghold, your shepherd, your counselor, your friend, your redeemer, your Saviour, your guide? If He is, you don't need to search any further for security.[8]

If you do not already know her story, you will soon discover the trials Elisabeth Elliot endured that earned her the right to speak this outstanding truth.

On days when you can barely breathe because of the pain, acknowledge briefly in your mind: "God loves me with an everlasting love. He is real. His Word is true. He keeps His promises." Sometimes I have done this all throughout my day. This simple acknowledgment is a beautiful surrendering act of worship. *"Those who sow in tears shall reap with shouts of joy!"* (Psalm 126:5). Acknowledging God's sovereignty in the midst of suffering will fertilize the seed of hope in your heart.

Trust His power, the Holy Spirit in you, to strengthen you day by day. Cry out to Him. Cling to Him. Saturate your mind in the Word. (Try reading the Psalms in troublesome times.) Rest in the knowledge that *experiencing pain can absolutely bring about a greater experience of joy.* You do not have to manufacture your joy. There is no burden that you must pick up in your grief in order to feel joy again. He will complete the work He began in You. Rest in God today, friend.

What Part of Your Story Threatens to Rob Today's Joy?

Read the following list and consider which of these challenges might be a threat to your joy.

Poverty	Gluttony	Witchcraft
Abuse	Complacency	Jealousy
Racism	Laziness	Drunkenness
Rejection	Lying	Pride
Abortion	Death	Selfishness
Sexual immorality	Loss	Disappointment
Greed	Idolatry	

As you evaluate your joy-robbers, let's re-visit the name for God in the Bible that describes Him as the God who sees. He is El Roi. He is full of compassion and His mercy never fails. He is gracious, slow to anger. He is generous in forgiveness. He is fully good. He sees your struggles and He will carry you through them.

He Sees You

To the woman who must put her children to bed hungry, He sees you.

To the woman who is fatherless and motherless, He sees you.

To the woman who grieves the child she buried, He sees you.

To the woman who chases sexual fulfillment, He sees you.

To the woman who turns to food to suppress her feelings, He sees you.

To the lonely and grieving widow, He sees you.

To the woman who feels marginalized by society, He sees you.

To the woman who gave her life away for too long, He sees you.

To the woman who drinks alcohol until the world fades away, He sees you.

To the woman who has been ravaged by abuse, He sees you.

To the woman who aborted her baby, He sees you.

To the woman who feels confused and overwhelmed, He sees you.

To the woman who feels she has nothing to show for her life, He sees you.

To the woman who is paralyzed physically or spiritually, He sees you.

To the woman who lied to achieve success, He sees you.

To the woman who desperately needs relief, He sees you.

To the woman who wants everything she does not have, He sees you.

To the woman grieving a prodigal child, He sees you.

To the woman who is raising her grandchildren, He sees you.

To the woman whose husband left, He sees you.

To the woman battling an unending illness, He sees you.

To the woman who just kissed her soldier goodbye, He sees you.

To the woman who waits for love, He sees you.

He sees you and He loves you with everlasting love.

He is Adonai, the Lord. He is Elohim, the Creator, the Beginning and the End. He is El Elyon, God Most High. He is El Shaddai, All Sufficient One. He is Jehova, the Self-Existent One. He is Jehova-Jirah, the Lord Will Provide. He is Jehova-Rapha, the Lord that Heals. He promises to bring good out of every situation. He is unchanging for eternity. He is all-powerful, all-knowing and everywhere, always. He is the ultimate judge.

You do not have to be a slave to your sin. He offers you forgiveness—for free. When you repent of your sin and accept His gift of salvation, He throws your sins away and does not remember them. *"As far as the east is from the west, so far does He remove our transgressions from us"* (Psalm 103:12). Dear one, do not be ensnared with that for which you are already forgiven. Once you have repented of your sin and asked for forgiveness from God, He does exactly as He says He will—He forgives you! He does not lie. He keeps His promises.

There is no shame for the forgiven. You may grieve what might have been every now and then, friend, but let your hope and peace be found in the One who forgives and never ever, ever, ever, ever changes His mind or throws past sins in your face. He is pure and trustworthy. We know from Romans that *"There is therefore now no condemnation for those who are in Christ Jesus. For the law of the Spirit of life has set you free in Christ Jesus from the law of sin and death"* (Romans 8:1-2).

Yes, friends, some days we lose our joy. Sometimes life feels like a moment-by-moment battle. Whether through a life circumstance or a choice of the heart, the thieves of joy threaten to derail all of us. Refocus on the God Who sees, forgives and loves you. Then let Him use you in this world.

Surrounded by the constant buzz and demands of our culture, sometimes crippled by sorrow, priorities can slowly shift. I am guilty too. We can find ourselves completely invested in the hope of easier days, fulfilling relationships, dreamy weddings, fabulous houses, gourmet meals, beautifully edited wardrobes, happy times with our children and grandchildren, or a relaxing retirement. Maybe for you the culprit is different, but the point is the same. These things in and of themselves are not evil, but when we invest our hearts into them and look to them for satisfaction, something is wrong. Meanwhile (and I am not trying to be cliché here—stick with me), real children today are being raped and are starving and freezing to death all over the world. Let us seek God's will as we pursue meeting the many needs in the world. We must not neglect prayerfully exploring what God wants to do with this powerful joy we have found in Him.

The fastest way to lose your joy is to keep it to yourself.

Chapter 9
Refreshed Joy

"Do you often feel like parched ground, unable to produce anything worthwhile? I do. When I am in need of refreshment, it isn't easy to think of the needs of others. But I have found that if, instead of praying for my own comfort and satisfaction, I ask the Lord to enable me to give to others, an amazing thing often happens—I find my own needs wonderfully met. Refreshment comes in ways I would never have thought of, both for others, and then, incidentally, for myself."
– Elisabeth Elliot[1]

Elisabeth Elliot is an amazing woman of faith who set an inspiring example of serving God diligently and spreading the Gospel, despite her difficult circumstances. She joyfully proclaimed the name of Jesus to the end of her life. Yet, even she sometimes felt "like parched ground, unable to produce anything worthwhile."

Remember, as believers, we are saints called to live a life that is set apart to God. Our walks with Christ are a process of growing in holiness. That process is possible by the power of the Spirit at work in us. We will never achieve perfection on this earth. Despite even the best of efforts, we sometimes lose our joy as distractions, dry times, trials, crises, grief and depression threaten to derail us. Thankfully, we have a known path back to joy.

1. **Redeemed** – Think on your salvation and your Savior.

2. **Renewed** – Trust the Holy Spirit's power at work in and through you.

3. **Relationship** – Abide in God. Fill your heart and mind with His Word and spend time in prayer.

4. **Re-Purposed** – Reach out to others with the love of God. The quote from Elisabeth Elliot at the beginning of this chapter illustrates this thought beautifully: "But I have found that if, instead of praying for my own comfort and satisfaction, I ask the Lord to enable me to give to others, an amazing thing often happens—I find my own needs wonderfully met."

5. **Re-Focus** – Give thanks to God in all circumstances. Even during hard times, we can thank Him for promising never to leave us and for giving us the Bible to refresh our hearts and lead us in His way.

Elisabeth Elliot endured painful trials for the sake of bringing the Gospel to unreached people. Her legacy has greatly impacted me because she joyfully proclaimed her confident trust in Christ to the end of her days on Earth.

Elliot shared:

> A year after I went to Ecuador, Jim Elliot, whom I had met at Wheaton, also entered tribal areas with the Quichua Indians. In nineteen fifty-three we were married in the city of Quito and continued our work together. Jim had always hoped to have the opportunity to enter the territory of an unreached tribe. The Aucas were in that

category—a fierce group whom no one had succeeded in meeting without being killed. After the discovery of their whereabouts, Jim and four other missionaries entered Auca territory. After a friendly contact with three of the tribe, they were speared to death.

Our daughter Valerie was 10 months old when Jim was killed. I continued working with the Quichua Indians when, through a remarkable providence, I met two Auca women who lived with me for one year. They were the key to my going in to live with the tribe that had killed the five missionaries. I remained there for two years.[2]

In reading Elisabeth's story, I was impressed with her courageous obedience and God's power at work in her. He strengthened her to do a very hard job, to risk her own life in order to share the Gospel with the very people who killed her husband and father of her baby daughter. Honestly, it is a little hard to believe that even a woman so bold as Elisabeth Elliot could feel "unable to produce anything worthwhile." Her vulnerable statement points us to a freeing truth: We do not have to stay in those dry times. There is a way to refreshed joy.

The Joy Of The Lord Is Your Strength

The joy of the Lord = strength (Nehemiah 8:10). According to Merriam-Webster's Dictionary, "strength is the quality that allows someone to deal with problems in a determined and effective way."[3] We have a job to do with this joy we have discovered!

Remember, the fastest way to lose your joy is to keep it to yourself. Renew your heart and mind in the Word of God and trust the Holy Spirit to empower and enable you. Engage in relationship with others, and you will begin to find that people are broken and hurting in your community and across the world. You will sense the Spirit's leading to minister to others through the special gifts He has given you.

I had a special opportunity to serve people far from my home in Alaska. Landing in Moscow initiated a life-changing experience. On this trip with SOAR International Ministries, we assisted local churches in delivering Christmas Stockings filled with toys, treats, essential hygiene items and a Russian children's Bible to many different orphanages. At each stop, we had opportunities to share the Gospel and interact one-on-one with the orphans and their caregivers.

My worldview was rocked to the core as I faced need in a whole new way. Beyond the basic needs of these children, what greatly impacted me was that so many of these orphans and street children had no one to wrap them in a hug each morning and love them with a forever kind of love. Beyond the need for socks and toothpaste, who would whisper to them that God made them and loves them and has a plan for them?

As I traveled through the orphanages, I had a pocket filled with shimmering green ribbons. Little girls would line up as I sat cross-legged on the floor for hours and tied their hair in braids and bows. I had no idea that the children would flock to me for such a simple little gift, but oh, how they longed to be hugged and loved, to feel gentle hands slowly combing through tangles and tying up a braid.

One little girl in particular looked exactly like me as a child. The similarities were uncanny. With all of my heart I wished I could bring that precious girl home with me. In seeing her picture now with that little green bow tied in her hair, I am reminded of God's mercy and deliverance, how He has so gently lifted me out of my sorrow and given me the opportunity now to reach out with His love to a hurting world.

Persevering Joy

The Spirit of the Lord God is upon me, because the Lord has anointed me to bring good news to the poor; He has sent me to bind up the brokenhearted, to proclaim liberty to the captives, and the opening of the prison to those who are bound; to proclaim the year of the Lord's favor, and the day of vengeance of our God; to comfort all who mourn; to grant to those who mourn in Zion—to give them a beautiful headdress instead of ashes, the oil of gladness instead of mourning, the garment of praise instead of a faint spirit; that they may be called oaks of righteousness, the planting of the Lord, that He may be glorified. (Isaiah 61:1-3)

This passage gives me chills. Isaiah the prophet describes the coming Christ. Jesus Himself read aloud some of this very prophesy while in the synagogue in Nazareth (Luke 4:18-19). Over the past five years, my heart has gone from shattered to healed, from weak to purposeful, from insecure to knowing lasting and powerful joy. It is as though I have been given wings and a message that needs to be shared. This became my prayer as I read Isaiah 61:

Lord, by Your strength I will,

- bring the Good News to the poor (in heart and physical need),

- bind up the brokenhearted as other dear women have reached out to minister to me in times of brokenness,

- proclaim liberty to captives of sin and open the door of their prison to a life of freedom in Christ,

- proclaim the year of the Lord's favor and also the day of vengeance of our God that none might perish,

- comfort those who mourn with the oil of gladness and joy, and

- offer the garment of praise in trade for a faint spirit,

"that they may be called oaks of righteousness, the planting of the Lord, that He may be glorified."

That He may be glorified... Not so that my whole life will be happy and fun. Not so that I will ultimately be delighted by every way that I get to serve Christ. Not for me at all, but for His glory.

Sometimes—often—ministry is extremely hard. To help us through the difficulty, we have the peace that comes with obeying God's leading and we have the power of the Holy Spirit to do what He calls us to do. We will have to make sacrifices as we continually learn to die to self and become more like Jesus, but they are totally worth it. David Livingston spent many years facing tremendous trials for the sake of the Gospel in Africa. Regarding eternal perspective and his role as a missionary, Livingston said:

> For my own part, I have never ceased to rejoice that God has appointed me to such an office. People talk of the sacrifice I have made in spending so much of my life in Africa... Is that a sacrifice which brings its own blest reward in healthful activity, the consciousness of doing good, peace of mind, and a bright hope of a glorious destiny hereafter? Away with the word in such a view, and with such a thought! It is emphatically no sacrifice. Say rather it is a privilege. Anxiety, sickness, suffering, or danger, now and then, with a foregoing of the common conveniences and charities of this life, may make us pause, and cause the spirit to waver, and the soul to sink; but let this only be for a moment. All these are nothing when compared with the glory which shall be revealed in and for us. *I never made a sacrifice.*[4]

By the power of the Spirit at work in us, unto the glory of God, may we, like David Livingston, persevere with joy in the calling that God places on our lives.

> *Moreover [let us also be full of joy now!] let us exult and triumph in our troubles and rejoice in our sufferings, knowing that pressure and affliction and hardship produce patient and unswerving endurance. And endurance (fortitude) develops maturity of character (approved faith and tried integrity). And character [of this sort] produces [the habit of] joyful and confident hope of eternal salvation.* (Romans 5:3-4, AMP)

By God's strength, friend, faithfully endure distress, pressure and trouble. Celebrate the patient endurance, spiritual maturity, hope and confident assurance of salvation that results from joyful perseverance. Regardless of circumstances, the life that abides in Christ will always have *purpose*, *power* and a *path* to refreshed joy.

Chapter 10
Joy Changes Everything

"Like the wind, Grace finds us wherever we are and won't leave us however we were found."
– Ann Voskamp[1]

Discovering the path to joy changes you, impacts the people in your sphere of influence and overflows into the world around you. When you have placed your life in the hands of God, walk by the Spirit, abide in His Word, reach out with His love to those around you and live a life of continual gratitude, then your eyes will begin to see life in a new way. Pain and blessings both become gifts. You can have joy, regardless of your circumstances, because of the One in whom your joy is found. You cannot manufacture joy and you do not have to fake it. Powerful and lasting joy is found in the Lord alone.

This path to joy in the Lord has changed my life. Though I am still learning and growing, I have a strengthened faith, more confident peace, inspired purpose and a bold trust in God. He has opened my eyes to the joy of life in Him. His joy trickles down into all areas of my life, extending to my husband, children, friends and beyond. His joy inspires happiness and gratitude throughout my days. His joy allows me to see every single day as a gift. The joy of the Lord can change your life too.

As you finish this book and move forward on your journey, I would like to remind you once again of the free gifts waiting for you at www.pageofjoy.com/bookgift. Included are some powerful tools that will help you return to joy again and again. I hope these gifts are a blessing in your life as they have been in mine.

Closing

Dear one, nothing in life will bring you ultimate joy outside of the deeply satisfying love of Jesus. Choose today to be redeemed, recognizing and believing that He gave His perfect life up on the cross as a sacrifice for your sins. He died in your place and desires that you accept salvation today. Choose eternal life with Him. Repent of your sins and choose to follow after Him wholeheartedly, if you have not already. He wants to wash you clean of sin and shame and make you alive in Him. He gives hope and purpose to your life that will bring glory to His name—what joy!

Believers in Jesus, do not let this be said of you: *"But I have this against you, that you have abandoned the love you had at first"* (Revelation 2:4). When life is hard and trials hit, always remember, *"the joy of the Lord is your strength"* (Nehemiah 8:10).

Nothing can separate you from the love of Jesus.

> *...we are more than conquerors and gain a surpassing victory through Him who loved us. For I am persuaded beyond doubt (am sure) that neither death nor life, nor angels nor principalities, nor things impending and threatening nor things to come, nor powers, nor height nor depth, nor anything else in all creation will be able to separate us from the love of God, which is in Christ Jesus our Lord.* (Romans 8:37-39, AMP)

Follow the path to joy in the Lord. *God is real, His Word is true and He keeps every one of His promises.*

"...for You have been my help,
and in the shadow of Your wings
I will sing for joy."
(Psalm 63:7)

It is my prayer that through reading

this book you have discovered the true

source of lasting and powerful joy!

If you have been encouraged by

these words then please leave a

review on Amazon.com. Your review

will help to spread the Gospel

and the joy of the Lord!

Because of His great love,

STEPHANIE JOY PAGE is a follower of Jesus. With a heart for encouraging women in the Lord, she blogs regularly at pageofjoy.com. God has done a great work in her life and she desires to see other women experience the same healing, peace, purpose, hope and joy in Him! Stephanie, her husband and children reside in a quaint Alaskan town.

Notes

INTRODUCTION

1. "Happiness" and "joy." Merriam-Webster.com. 2016. Online: http:// www.merriam-webster.com (July 30, 2016).

CHAPTER 1: REDEEMED

1. Nicole C. Mullen, "Redeemer," *Redeemer* (Warner/Chappell Music, Inc., 2000).

2. Dave Anderson, "Plane Down In The Bering Sea," *Christianity Today* (September/October 1996), 28.

3. Don Wharton, "The Rescue." Online: http://donwharton. com/rescue.htm (July 4, 2016).

4. John Newton, "Amazing Grace," *Olney Hymns* (1779), 53-54.

CHAPTER 2: RENEWED

1. A.W. Tozer, *The Pursuit of God*, Kindle Edition (Franklin, NC: Christian Miracle Foundation Press, 2011), 35.

2. "Joy." James Orr, et al., eds., *International Standard Bible Encyclopedia*. 1939. Online: http:// Internationalstandardbible.com (July 17, 2016).

3. C.S. Lewis, *Mere Christianity* (San Francisco: Zondervan, 2001), 38-39.

CHAPTER 3: RELATIONSHIP

1. C.T. Studd, "Only One Life, Twill Soon Be Past." Found online at Paul Hockley, "Quote: Only One Life, Twill Soon Be Past – Poem by C.T Studd," Paul Hockley (blog). http:// paulhockley.com/2016/05/24/quote-only-one-life-twill-soon-be-past-poem-by-c-t-studd/ (July 25, 2016).

2. "Meno." James Strong, *Strong's Exhaustive Concordance of the Bible*. 2016. Found online at: https://www.blueletterbible.org/lang/lexicon/lexicon.cfm?Strongs=G3306&t=KJV (July 30, 2016).

3. "Nourish." Merriam-Webster.com. 2016. Online: http://www.merriam-webster.com (July 30, 2016).

4. "Holy." W.E. Vine, Merrill F. Unger, William White, Jr., 1940. *Vine's Complete Expositional Dictionary of Old and New Testament Words*. Online: http://www.menfak.no/bibelprog/vines.pl?word=holy (July 30, 2016).

CHAPTER 4: REPURPOSED

1. Sally Lloyd-Jones, *The Jesus Storybook Bible: Every Story Whispers His Name* (Grand Rapids, Michigan: Zondervan, 2007), 126.

2. Ron Hutchcraft, *A Life That Matters* (Chicago, IL: Moody Publishers, 2007), 67.

CHAPTER 5: RE-FOCUS

1. Ann Voskamp, "Being joyful isn't what makes you grateful... being grateful is what makes you joyful." October 9, 2014, 4:45 PM. Tweet.

2. Jonathan Parnell, "Living in the Valley—For Now," Desiring God (blog), April 8, 2013. http://www.desiringgod.org/articles/living-in-the-valley-for-now.

3. "Hypomonē." James Strong, *Strong's Exhaustive Concordance of the Bible*. 2016. Found online at: https://www.blueletterbible.org/lang/lexicon/lexicon.cfm?Strongs=G5281&t= (July 25, 2016).

CHAPTER 6: ENDURANCE

1. A.W. Tozer, *The Pursuit of God*, Kindle Edition (Franklin, NC: Christian Miracle Foundation Press, 2011), 18.

2. Ibid., 20.

CHAPTER 7: PULLING IT ALL TOGETHER

1. A.W. Tozer, *The Pursuit of God*, Kindle Edition (Franklin, NC: Christian Miracle Foundation Press, 2011), 57.

CHAPTER 8: HOW TO LOSE YOUR JOY

1. Elisabeth Elliot, *Waiting. Keep A Quiet Heart.* (Ann Arbor, MI: Vine Books, 1995), 135.

2. Theodore Roosevelt, "Comparison is the thief of joy."

3. Dee Brestin, *Idol Lies* (Franklin, TN: Worthy Publishing, 2012), 48.

4. Ann Voskamp, "How to Find Happiness in the Dark," A Holy Experience (blog), March 11, 2013. http://www.aholyexperience.com/2013/03/how-to-find-happiness-in-the-dark/ (August 10, 2016).

5. Ann Voskamp, "Only the Good Stuff: Multivitamins for Your Weekend," A Holy Experience (blog), June 28, 2014. http://www.aholyexperience.com/2014/06/only-the-good-stuff-multivitamins-for-your-weekend-06-28-14/ (August 10, 2016).

6. "Happiness" and "joy." Merriam-Webster.com. 2016. Online: http:// www.merriam-webster.com (July 30, 2016).

7. Elisabeth Elliot, "I am not a theologian or a scholar, but I am very aware of the fact that pain is necessary to all of us. In my own life, I think I can honestly say that out of the deepest pain has come the strongest conviction of the presence of God and the love of God." Found online

at: Jacqueline, "Elisabeth Elliot: Her Life, Books, and Best Quotes," Deep Roots at Home (blog), June 18, 2015. http://deeprootsathome.com/elisabeth-elliot-her-life-books-and-best-quotes/ (August 9, 2016).

8. Elisabeth Elliot, "Where does your security lie? Is God your refuge, your hiding place, your stronghold, your shepherd, your counselor, your friend, your redeemer, your saviour, your guide? If He is, you don't need to search any further for security." Found online at: "Elisabeth Ellitot Quotes," Women Of Christianity (blog), June 17, 2015. http://womenofchristianity.com/quotes/elisabeth-elliot-quotes/ (June 29, 2016).

CHAPTER 9: REFRESHED JOY

1. Elisabeth Elliot, *A Lamp Unto My Feet: The Bible's Light for Your Daily Walk* (Ann Arbor, MI: Vine Books, 1985), 16.

2. Elisabeth Elliot, "About Elisabeth," Elisabeth Elliot. Online: http:// elisabethelliot.org/about.html (July 4, 2016).

3. "Strength." Merriam-Webster.com. 2016. Online: http://www.merriam-webster.com (July 30, 2016).

4. David Livingston, Untitled. Published in Gloria Furman, *Treasuring Christ When Your Hands are Full* (Wheaton, IL: Crossway, 2014), 91.

CHAPTER 10: JOY CHANGES EVERYTHING

1. Ann Voskamp, "When You've Been Looking for a Sign," A Holy Experience (blog), April 10, 2015. Online: http://www.aholyexperience.com/2015/04/when-youve-been-looking-for-a-sign/ (August 9, 2016).

CPSIA information can be obtained
at www.ICGtesting.com
Printed in the USA
LVOW11s1940091017

551764LV00003B/791/P